The NEXT STEP

A Guide to Balanced Recovery

The NEXT STEP

A Guide to Balanced Recovery

TODD WEBER

Seattle, Washington

Published by Glen Abbey Books, Inc.

Cover design by:
     Graphiti, Inc.
     Seattle, Washington

Library of Congress Cataloging-in-Publication Data

Weber, Todd A.
  The next step : a guide to balanced recovery / Todd A. Weber. — 1st ed.
        p.   cm.
     ISBN 0-934125-25-2 : $8.95
     1. Spiritual life. 2. Gratitude. 3. Self-actualization (Psychology). 4.
Twelve-step programs. I. Title.
BL624.W384   1991   91-32096
                                                                  CIP

First Edition
ISBN 0-934125-25-2
Printed in the United States of America

10 9 8 7 6 5 4 3 2 1

For Irene,

An instrument of my fate ...

With Love

Contents

Acknowledgment

Special thanks to the following for their support and help: the Workgroup, Trinity, and all my clients for the acceptance and willingness to be my teachers; Bill Pittman, Linda McClelland, and Kelly Pensell for all the wonderful editing, artwork, and education; my homegroup, S.O.S., and Terry for being there all this time; my friend Wolf for help when it counted; and my family, for all the lessons learned.

Introduction

This book is the result of an insight. The insight came about through many different events, experiences, and studies combining to produce the explosion of awareness and grace that happened. I will explain the history of this awareness and give some exercises that helped me. The rest will be up to you.

I received the gift of **knowing** that for some people, including me, the quickest and easiest way to grow spiritually, emotionally, financially, and any other way I could think of is through gratitude—as appreciation, praise, acknowledgment, thanksgiving, surrender, prayer, and practice.

This book is about how to practice gratitude and how to make your life an arena for expansion and growth. I have outlined exercises and the original insight in the companion book to this one, *The Next Step Workbook*.

I originally thought that I would aim this book at recovering people from all the Twelve Step programs, the ACOA movement, and all the other recovery movements. John Bradshaw estimates that up to 96% of us come from dysfunctional backgrounds, so almost all of us fit into one of those categories. This book definitely *will* help those of you in those groups. I am in 12 Step recovery myself and can identify very much with the pain and difficulty of moving into health.

However, this book has a much bigger application than just for those in recovery. It is for all who want to become more: more healthy, more giving, more spiritually connected, more complete, and more in line with the meaning and purpose of their lives.

There will be many references to the Twelve Steps and the groups associated with them. Not all of them will be flattering. I have gone through many changes over the past ten-plus years working a program, and some of the time I was angry, rebellious, in denial, and stubborn. Some of the writing will reflect that. Other times I was clear and insightful. Some of the writing will reflect that as well.

I ask you to keep an open mind and heart. I may say some things that will challenge you or make you sensitive. Please try to hang in there—take what you can use, and leave the rest. Just remember that originally I was aiming this book at those in recovery, and broadened the scope as it became apparent to me that gratitude is a gift for everyone who is willing to take a look at it.

One method for using this book and exploring the concepts presented is to keep it very simple. So many books on growth and recovery are convoluted exercises in the author's theory written in difficult, academic language. There are some wonderful exceptions to this, some of which I will be quoting in this work, but most are either written for scholarly purposes or are too esoteric to be practical.

This work is simple. Gratitude is very straightforward. All the discussion and tangents we will explore can be ignored, if you choose to. The important thing is to practice gratitude. Remember—keep it simple. That doesn't mean it's easy!

All the profoundly affecting truths are simple. Like an arrow to the heart, the spiritual truths and universal laws are immediate and make sense. Trust your intuition and heart. Try not to make this an exercise in the intellect, but a discovery of the soul.

Another reminder I want to give you is to be gentle. We are usually kinder to strangers than we are to ourselves. Let this book work gently with you. Don't judge or criticize your progress or lack of it. It is not about results.

Be gentle in your approach to this work and in viewing yourself. Be open to forgiveness of yourself and others. Know that we will be pushing a lot of buttons that cause reaction rather than response. Be gentle with yourself until you can move past the reaction to the response, for it is in the response that the growth occurs, and the reaction gives us the direction in which to move for the fastest growth.

So both reaction and response are necessary. Don't judge yourself because of how you feel or react or respond. Just be aware. We will be working with all of it!

One more thing to be aware of: I am in recovery myself, as we will discuss throughout the book. I have been given the gift of insight in one area of my life. I wish to share that with you. In all areas of my life, I am still learning and growing. I have blind spots and numbness that I haven't found yet. When you come across any of these in the book, be gentle with me. Know that I am on the journey, too. I am a teacher, not a guru or a saint. This teaching is expanding and enlarging me, even as I write.

I ask you to be a student, not a follower. Question what you read and question the exercises, but question them *after* you have read the book and *after* you have done the exercises.

Growth comes from doing. Give yourself an opportunity to expand through doing. Be gentle if it takes you awhile to do it, but do it! We will be exploring some hard and sensitive areas in your life. I have tried to give examples from my own life or one of my students' experiences to help guide you in the pursuit of growth. The effort must be yours, however.

Please accept this book in the spirit in which it is given: a gift, for opening and experiencing the unlimited nature of our lives through expansion into awareness and realization of God's love.

I have spent many years going to Twelve Step meetings and have many good memories and experiences from those meetings. The Twelve Step program is very good, but many people do not fully relate to all aspects of the program. After spending some time working the Steps, I was not getting the direction and guidance I needed to continue growing and moving spiritually.

For all the talk of AA and the other Twelve Step programs (Al-Anon, NA, Overeaters Anonymous, ACOA, etc.) being spiritual, I have seen a lot of confusion and mixed signals being given to newcomers and oldtimers alike, as to the exact nature of spiritual growth and change. Part of this is that the programs have to be very careful to remain non-religious organizations.

This is not to say the Twelve Step programs don't help a lot of people—they certainly do! But recovery can be much more than abstinence and meetings. Many people, after a few years or a few months, grow discouraged in the program. They've handled their drinking or drugging or whatever, but they still have the same mental, emotional, and spiritual difficulties. Sometimes they even feel worse, since they no longer have their substance to buffer the pain.

In spite of working the Steps, staying dry or clean, and attending meetings, many of us remain confused, have money problems, relationship difficulties, depression, or emotional distress. The promises seem to elude us, even though we've given full effort to the Steps. As Bill W. pointed out in his famous 1958 *Grapevine* article, we haven't achieved **emotional sobriety**.

Many of us are looking for a way to expand our lives, to move beyond our current limits and become more. The methods and exercises we will be discussing are a help to everyone wanting to grow. I offer this gift without limits or restrictions in the hope that many of you will accept the teaching and expand with it. I hope that you will consider what is being offered and open yourself to the potential for becoming more. You will be delighted with the process. It has helped me, my friends in recovery, and my many workshop participants.

The Next Step is based on an experience of insight that I gained from practicing gratitude. We will explore that insight in depth. It is a practice based on **doing**–not understanding, knowing, learning, or believing. Its meaning becomes clear from doing. I highly recommend reading and practicing the exercises introduced in *The Next Step Workbook*.

The Journey Begins

Mighty things from small beginnings grow.
—John Dryden

I got sober in the beginning of 1981. My story up to that point was like many others' stories. I had a broken marriage, was fired from or left many jobs, had many unkept promises, many car violations, many petty criminal activities. Like most of us, I had lots of talent and potential. I just couldn't quite make it all come together.

Of course, I thought that if you had my problems, and my family, and my situation, you'd drink and drug the way I did. My life kept getting worse: feelings of depression and hopelessness, a failed attempt at suicide, a move to another state that ended in disaster. I reduced my life to pretty simple terms: the next drink, the money to get the one after that, and something or someone to help me forget the pain of existence.

I finally had enough. My brother helped get me into outpatient alcohol treatment, and my recovery began. The counselors at treatment were quick to point out that their help was just temporary, and that I needed to hook up with a recovery group in order to achieve any long-term results.

I started going to Twelve Step meetings right away. I met some great people who seemed to be able to laugh and have a good time, even though they weren't drinking and doping. They told me if I wanted to hang around with them I had to go to meetings, read the literature, do the Steps, and not drink today. I wanted to be like those guys, so I did the drill.

I wanted what they seemed to have—serenity, happiness in the face of problems, and the ability to talk about it without being caught by it. I started going to meetings almost every night. I read the Big Book. I started doing the Steps. I didn't drink today. My life started getting better.

It was great! Of course there were rough spots, here and there. I had lots of good people with whom to talk it through, and I wasn't drinking or using. For about two years, things went extremely well. I didn't make much progress in becoming any better in relationships, but the rest of my life improved dramatically. About a year and a half into sobriety, I quit smoking. I had been a three-or-more-packs-a-day person up to then. It felt great to be able to give it up!

I started running and taking better care of myself. I went back to school and tried some new things. I still had an addictive personality, with compulsive and obsessive behaviors, but I felt I was making tremendous progress. I was going to meetings almost every day.

I had a minor crisis of faith, and was helped through it by doing the 4th and 5th Steps. Things were going swimmingly. I got married again—and divorced again. I still didn't have the skills and maturity to handle relationships well. I ended up in counseling, working on anger and Third Step issues—letting go and letting God. It started becoming apparent to me that my understanding of the Steps and the program didn't help everything.

I was searching for a spiritual identity and not having much luck in the program. Although there is much talk of spirituality in the Twelve Step programs, I found little practical help. It is a frustrating and disheartening experience to be told often and loudly that it is a spiritual program, yet to see only limited approaches to spiritual paths, and not much tolerance for non-Christian traditions. Looking outside the program or getting help from a counselor was the same as stating that the program was a failure. I think that attitude has changed dramatically in the past few years, thank God, but it was fairly prevalent at the time.

I went to a therapist. I devoured books on spirituality. I meditated, prayed, and contemplated. I went to classes. I discovered a strange thing: the more I searched and looked and worked on spirituality, the further alcohol moved away from being an issue. By not concentrating entirely on meeting attendance, my recovery was getting stronger. I was working on "real" issues like relationships, not avoiding them by going to meetings and concentrating on my obsessive and compulsive behavior. I was dealing with reality on a moment-to-moment basis.

When I attended Twelve Step meetings, I couldn't believe some of what I would hear. It didn't seem possible to me that people could still be talking about the same problems and issues that had been bothering them five, six, or seven years before. Granted, many people were making tremendous progress, but many weren't or were stymied in their desire to grow.

I had become so frustrated that I did not talk about my confusion at meetings any more. It always seemed to turn into an argument. Few in the Twelve Step programs were open to looking at other solutions or possible improvements, I thought. I saw the problem as being stuck in two-stepping the program, just attending meetings and staying abstinent.

My life began to get better with the help of Twelve Step groups. It continued to get better outside of the program. When I stopped confusing meeting attendance as working the program, as I saw many doing, I began to integrate the program into my life. Now, when I attend meetings, I talk about my struggles and progress with spiritual issues.

Through an active and textured spiritual life, I have gained some awareness that I know will help others. It doesn't matter if you are a drunk or addicted or codependent or ACOA or "normal." All of us have self-worth and self-esteem issues. At their core, all addictive and compulsive behaviors have low self-esteem as their breeding ground.

I have found a way to work directly with self-esteem, without any mumbo-jumbo or tricks or having to find "it," just straightforward experience from *doing*. We will spend the rest of the book discussing this method.

The Twelve Steps

For those of you unfamiliar with the Twelve Step programs, let's take a quick look at the Twelve Steps. I will make some comments about each Step. These comments are expanded in other parts of the book. The overall premise is the Steps were put together by the first 100 people in A.A. to get sober. Many feel they were divinely inspired.

> **Step 1:** *We admitted we were powerless over alcohol (drugs, food, sex, alcoholics, etc) — that our lives had become unmanageable.*

Surrender, a complete giving up, is the basis for getting better in the program. The spiritual concept of surrender is often misunderstood in our society. We'll discuss it in some depth later.

> **Step 2:** *Came to believe that a Power greater than ourselves could restore us to sanity.*

After surrender, then we must admit that it takes a power greater than ourselves to "make" us better, that without divine intervention we are helpless and defeated. This can be a confusing stumbling block for some. The concept of grace and the importance of personal accountability are intertwined in this Step.

Step 3: *Made a decision to turn our will and our lives over to the care of God* **as we understood Him.**

Here is the "let go and let God" part of the program, putting our life back in God's hands. (When was it ever out?) We will discuss this step in detail in terms of the will and God's greatest gift to us.

Step 4: *Made a searching and fearless moral inventory of ourselves.*

This is often an impossibility for a person with limited or low self-esteem. Fear is one of the major problems, yet it can be a driving force for change at the same time that it causes the most resistance.

Step 5: *Admitted to God, to ourselves, and to another human being the exact nature of our wrongs.*

When we are "being a behavior," caught up in acting it out, it is very difficult to see the behavior. To be able to categorize the exact nature of our wrongs is difficult, and to label them as "wrong" is to negate the lessons and gifts available to us from examination of them in the light of gratitude. My most difficult experiences have given me the greatest gifts.

Step 6: *Were entirely ready to have God remove all these defects of character.*

Again, this is an amazing shift in accountability for our behavior.

Step 7: *Humbly asked Him to remove our shortcomings.*

As we will discuss, maybe a more appropriate prayer is for the will to make a decision to change our own shortcomings. It appears to me that God's will is manifest!

Step 8: *Made a list of all persons we had harmed, and became willing to make amends to them all.*

We will discuss this Step and the next in the context of forgiveness, with the emphasis on being accountable.

Step 9: *Made direct amends to such people wherever possible, except when to do so would injure them or others.*

Again, we will be looking at accountability and forgiveness when we discuss this Step.

Step 10: *Continued to take personal inventory and when we were wrong promptly admitted it.*

An inventory is a great tool to help with change. Perhaps, instead of judging behavior and labeling ourselves, we might also use the inventory process to track change and improvement.

Step 11: *Sought through prayer and meditation to improve our conscious contact with God* **as we understood Him,** *praying only for knowledge of His will for us and the power to carry that out.*

This is a very interesting Step which we will discuss later at great length.

Step 12: *Having had a spiritual awakening as the result of working these Steps, we tried to carry this message to alcoholics (co-dependents, addicts, etc.), and to practice these principles in all our affairs.*

Part of the difficulty of the program, and why so few people actually stick with it (relative to the number of people who start Twelve Step programs), is that the Steps are sometimes hard to understand and difficult to practice. We tend to think they are the total answer, or not the answer at all. That "all or nothing" thinking is very typical of addictive people.

I invite you to take a new look at the Steps. Consider looking at concepts outside them and outside of recovery. Open yourself to the possibility of further growth. Wholeness is a difficult concept for all of us. Man has been searching for a path to spiritual wholeness for ages.

Let's look at ways to move beyond the Steps, into a spiritual dimension of growth and expansion that pulls us into health and unlimited living. As Bill W. talked about in his article on "Emotional Sobriety," alcohol (drugs, food, sex, gambling) is just a symptom. It is the underlying "dis-ease" that needs to be addressed. Stopping the addictive practice isn't enough. Stopping the behavior that hurts or confuses us isn't the total answer. We must grow into a new way of being. Let's take *The Next Step* in moving toward becoming whole, spiritual beings.

The Twelve Steps are reprinted with permission of A.A. World Services, Inc., New York, New York.

Gratitude

He is a wise man who does not grieve for the things which he has not, but rejoices for those which he has.

—*Epictetus*

Gratitude is the quickest path to God. It is a direct method of spiritual awakening. It gives us a way to become more, have more, give more, know more, and grow more, all very simply and directly. Gratitude is a practice that can expand all experience. It is the fastest way to the Higher Self and direct experience of the flow of creation and the bounty of the universe. (In the section on will, we'll discuss the Higher Self in more detail.)

Gratitude is mentioned in the Twelve Step programs for the month of November, but no Step addresses it directly and no directions or methods are given for practicing it. *It is very important.*

I was given a gift of insight through gratitude. It became apparent to me that gratitude is the simplest, most direct path to raising self-esteem. Through this practice everything gets better. Spiritual growth accelerates to warp speed and stays there.

Practicing gratitude, through the use of the will and forgiveness, also implies direct accountability for our lives, where we are now, and how we got here, with no blame, no excuses, no laying it off on disease or dysfunction. We can look for the lessons in the experience, and let it go, but not to lay it on someone else's doorstep.

Practicing gratitude starts with a very simple exercise. We will do some exercises during the course of this book, because growth is not about knowing, or learning, or understanding, or believing—it is about *doing!* (See *The Next Step Workbook* by this author for further discussion of gratitude and many more exercises for developing growth.) We often don't need to know or understand completely, we just need to *do* in order to change and grow.

Start each morning with this very simple exercise: when you wake up, grab a piece of paper and a pen or pencil and start making a list of all your blessings, all the things that you are grateful for today: family, friends, breath, health, opportunity, senses, warmth, love, books, reading, growth, change, experiences, and so on. It will be different each day. Just list those things that you are aware you have gratitude for. Some days the list will be very short, as you may not be feeling well or in a good mood. Other days the list may be very long, as you have a lot to be grateful for. Just do the list every day for a minimum of two weeks to a month. Like this:

> *Thank God and the universe for light. For warmth and contrast, for being able to see. For color and brightness. For shape and form.*
>
> *Thank God and the universe for sound. For music and laughter. For high screech and low moan. For sweet baby's cry and blast of horn.*
>
> *Thank God and the universe for touch. For soft silk and skin and hard surfaces and sandpaper. For warmth of a hug and gentleness of a kiss. For lazy pressure of clothes and touch of breeze on bare skin.*

Thank God and the universe for all the senses, of flavor and fragrance, of texture and sneeze. For fullness and appetite, hunger and longing.

Thank God and the universe for mind. For imagination and fantasy. For thinking and wondering. For knowing and learning.

Thank God and the universe for family. For lessons learned of love and acceptance and discipline and effort. For warmth and home and holidays and gifts. For hard times giving strength.

Thank God and the universe for friends. For leading and following. For acceptance and rejection. For the pain of growing and changing, becoming different and separate. For loyalty and strength.

Thank God and the universe for all the experiences, good and bad, that pushed and molded and shoved me into becoming. For all the gifts and lessons contained in each instant, each moment. Thank God.

Every day it will be different. Every day it will grow. Every day new awareness will pull at us. Practicing gratitude puts us in the now! I am using "the now" in a sharper focus than the Twelve Step concept of "one day at a time." Now, as used here, means being totally present in *this instant*, aware, focused, and alert. It can include the inclination to action: I can act *now*; I am aware *now*. By practicing gratitude, we are able to gain perspective on experience and see the good in everything. It is not always easy, but it works, if you do the exercise. As you progress, gratitude can become a daily meditation, and only on occasion will you need to make a list.

Twelve Step groups talk a lot about living a day at a time. Just don't drink today. Gratitude allows you to live an instant at a time! Totally in the now, caught in the infinity of the moment and aware of the good, growing and becoming, moment to moment.

We will be talking more about gratitude shortly. For now, put down the book and write out a list of your blessings. Right now! Don't go any further until you have done this.

Now, how do you feel? A little different? Maybe a little better? If you will do a list every day for a month, it will change your whole outlook on life. It is so direct and powerful, it's spooky.

Gratitude is the lever that flips us out of the past and into the now. We will not wallow in the excesses or pain of the past. It also keeps us from borrowing trouble from the future. True gratitude is always present.

There are many parts to the practice of gratitude. The first is becoming aware of all we have to be grateful for, expanding the awareness of gratitude every day until one day, it incorporates everything: receiving more, the ability to be more, see more, have more, give more, know more, the incomparable gift of the bounty of the universe. All of it.

Abundance is no longer an issue. Plenty is no longer a worry. We have it all now. Of course we do.

I first started making a daily Blessings list after hearing my mentor, Edith Stauffer, say that the fastest way to the Higher Self was through gratitude. It made sense to me to make it a practice and see what happened.

I couldn't believe it. Things started changing immediately. My attitude improved overnight. I started seeing the good in people and situations without having to reach for it. I started remaining in the now, much more often and easily. I started seeing that everything I thought I needed in life was already here.

A steady stream of insights started flowing into me. New understandings and awareness of things and issues that had troubled me for years started to emerge. I caught a glimpse of that special flow of the matrix of creation where there is no time or limits or being separate; where possibility and love and connectedness expand without end. The flow is a place of awareness, of realization that we're all connected and part of the same thing. I was the flow and it was me. I started to be able to reach that state regularly and remain in it for extended periods of time. I was overjoyed. I had to share this experience, and I found that other people could do the same thing with the practice of gratitude.

It may not come easily to you, just by practicing the list. We will be discussing the issues that get in the way, all those things dealing with low self-esteem: not deserving it all, being guilty, fearing having it all, and the ability to become all that we can be. We will be discussing forgiveness issues, self-esteem issues, and will issues not directly addressed by the Twelve Step programs, so we will have tools and means for direct change. It means no more excuses or blaming. Our life is in our own hands, to become what we will!

It is a big responsibility, and it is easy to shirk. Not too many people want to be in charge of their own lives. Who wants to accept full responsibility for where we are, right now? Not too many of us.

However, gratitude, will, and forgiveness show us ways to be all we can be, to reach as far as we can, and to become our potential. It is so exciting and wonderful! A way to be more, to move past addiction, compulsion, and fear, toward our Higher Power, awareness, and fulfillment; a way to gain awakening and go beyond our limits. It is important to understand that this is an adjunct to the Twelve Steps, not a replacement. We must do all we can with the Steps *and* move beyond them for further growth and development.

Give it a shot. What do you have to lose? Maybe there is an easier, softer way—if the work is done. Take a look at it and make up your own mind, but don't just look at it and read it. Do it! Practice it! It is only through *doing* that the meaning becomes apparent.

We will be coming back to gratitude in many different contexts, but gratitude practiced is all that is necessary. The rest helps put things in perspective. Other exercises give us tools for removing the emotional hooks, but gratitude is the path to freedom! Now! No more being hung up on compulsive, destructive behavior. No more fears holding us back, procrastinating and hesitating. No more inability to make a decision or making impulsive hasty decisions. Living totally in the present, infinite in its glory and bounty, ever expanding and growing. Becoming who we *can* become. Stretching! Extending our reach to God!

The Will

Will is to grace as horse is to rider.
—St. Augustine

The will is the most misunderstood and neglected part of the Twelve Step programs. It is our instrument for change. It allows us to draw upon the wisdom and power of the Higher Self to expand, grow, and move. The Higher Self is that part of us which is connected directly to the Source or our Higher Power. It could be called the "soul" or the "Self." It is our conduit to universal laws and higher awareness.

The will is God's greatest gift to us. The ability to choose is our freedom and our jail. We can fly to the outermost reaches of our potential, yet we are anchored by the responsibility for the choices. With the gift, comes the accountability.

God's will is manifest. "Let there be light. And there was light." There is no limit to God's will—it is! To pray for knowledge of God's will is a way to deny the gifts we've been given. God gave us this universe. God gave us this body and mind. God gave us will. We are the only creature with choices. We can choose to limit ourselves. A tree doesn't ask how high to grow. It just grows, as high and as strong as it can, given the environment and nurturing it receives. The elephant doesn't ask how much elephant to be. It grows, it becomes, according to the genetic potential it received.

Man is the only creature with choice. What an awesome gift! What a tremendous responsibility. God gave us unlimited potential. It is up to *us* what we do with it. It is not God's will that determines my life. *It is my will.* To look elsewhere is to belittle the extraordinary nature of the gift we received.

We can choose to become more, to grow, to give more, to move toward God, to be the most we can be, or we can settle for less, for comfort and conforming to others' ideas of what we "should" be. We can dull our minds and bodies with TV and bad food and no exercise, and blame the government, the economy, our parents, our education or lack of it, and lack of opportunity for where we are and who we are. We can be a product of our addictions, or we can choose to rise above them. *It is our choice.*

The will is the bridge to the Higher Self, that allows us to see beyond our limits. We are limited by our thinking, knowing, believing, experiencing, learning, and sensing to those things we can sense and know. If it is beyond our ken, it doesn't exist, so we are unable to move beyond our limits based on mind and knowledge. We need the larger perspective of the Higher Self. The will, with grace, is the instrument that allows us to move toward the Higher Self and God.

John Bradshaw, in his book *The Family* and the PBS series of the same name, as well as other researchers, talks about the "disabled will." In an addicted person, the will is disabled, or used solely to *will to will*, as Bradshaw points out. It can seem to be the only area in an addict's life where there is control. The same holds true for many others who come from dysfunctional situations.

This is a very limited view of the will. Roberto Assagioli, M.D., in his book *The Act of Will*, talks about the higher use of the will to move into connection with our Higher Self, and the unlimited vision and perspective it entails. Through the grace of God, even the disabled will of addicts can be used to make a "higher" choice.

Grace is available to us all. God doesn't pick out specific addicts or drunks or ACOAs and say "You can get sober or clean or healthy, but that person can't." Grace is available to all of us. It is our choice to decide to get help. Through grace, we have the ability to use our will to make that choice. It was our choice, however, not God's or some other higher power's decision on an individual basis. What a grandiose conception! What a delusion, to think that God would intervene individually in my case.

God supplies grace, so we can use the will when we are addicted or disabled to make a "higher" choice. It is our responsibility to make the choice!

A disabled will decides for others. A disabled will decides to change and control circumstances. No wonder there is frustration and anger in addiction. Your will decides for you! To try to control others, circumstances, or situations is to be grandiose or helpless, as Bradshaw suggests. The glory of free will is that it is an individual gift. I can choose to change. So can you.

I was working with a group of business people the first time I consciously used will statements to move into growth. The group was working on mission statements, then defining areas of growth for the next six months to a year. The areas targeted for growth were defined by will statements—a form of affirmation. Again, Edith Stauffer had suggested to me the format for using the will.

I worked out five will statements to practice. (An example is: *"I, Todd Weber, a child of God, will to comfortably grow and expand spiritually by giving 3 or 4 workshops on Unconditional Love and Forgiveness this year."*) I wrote the will statements out ten times every night for two weeks. My wrist and hand got sore from writing. I recorded the will statements on a cassette and listened to them in my car. I recited the will statements to a friend or my partner every day. (See *The Next Step Workbook* for an expanded definition and practice of this exercise.)

Within a very short period of time, major changes started happening in my life. My financial goal, which I had targeted to reach in three years, was reached in four months! In looking back, I realize that all those will statements were reached or surpassed within a year. Absolutely remarkable! Am I an exceptional case? No. The will is a powerful instrument for change, and when channeled in line with universal law, will bring about fantastic growth.

The will puts the power and focus of higher energy behind our choices. It allows us to commit, to be totally with our decisions, and to put into action our intent.

We invoke the will to move beyond our understanding. The power of a purpose, with a will supporting it, is unstoppable. The stories of Christ, Mohammed, and Mahatma Gandhi all show the power of purpose with a will!

Most of us are not used to taking full responsibility for our choices, so we are not used to the will. It takes practice, and a certain willingness to move beyond our fear.

Some of the issues that limit will and our ability to make good choices have to do with self-esteem. We have deep-seated beliefs about our worth. We feel we don't deserve to be more, have more, give more, grow more. "If you knew what I was really like, you probably wouldn't even talk to me." We have ideas about who and what we are that limit us. We have fears of letting others see us, and knowing us for who we truly are.

We have distorted our view of our place in the universe, and have diminished our own value. If we practice gratitude, it becomes apparent that we all have equal value. This is not intellectual knowledge or understanding. It is an experience from the practicing of gratitude.

We are all children of God, deserving and unlimited. We've all been given equal measure of opportunity and sorrow, pain and joy, problems and solutions, trouble and serenity. We may not have equal talent, intelligence, or physical stature, but that has been compensated for. We are all children of God, given this universe to play in. What we do with it is our choice. There are no favorites. It has been given equally. We are where we are by choice!

For some of us, that is a hard concept to grasp. However, look at it this way. If it is not a choice, then we have no hope of changing it ourselves. We will be victims of circumstance and chance—there is nothing we can do about it. If, on the other hand, we are here by choice, then we can choose to change! It means there is hope! There is possibility! There is potential! It doesn't have to be this way, if this way is not where we want to be.

Gratitude gives us the ability to see the good and gifts in our current situation, and allows us to move to make it better. We get the best of both worlds: the ability to accept and the ability to change.

The will is the instrument of change. We use it first to change our concept of deserving. We deserve it all. The universe, in its great expanse, has abundance and joy and grace and plenty for all. You deserve it. If you are not where you would choose to be, then change your concept of deserving first.

Take a minute to go back to your last gratitude exercise. (You have been doing your list every day, right?) Close your eyes and remember, without clinging or hanging on to any thoughts or ideas, those things, people, and situations you are most grateful for. What is it that gives you the most gratitude? Take a few minutes to decide the two or three things that give you the most to be grateful for.

You will take those blessings and develop deserve statements from them. For example, I am very grateful for the insight of gratitude and the practice that has developed. So I will make a "deserve" statement like this: *"I, Todd Weber, a child of God, deserve to increase the gratitude in my life through practice and sharing."*

Let's take a look at some of the elements of this statement. First, by including the phrase "a child of God," I've reminded myself and the universe that I am part of the flow and expansion available to us all. I've included the element for which I am grateful and which I would like to see expanded and continued, and I have included an element of sharing or giving back.

The importance of each of these elements will become apparent. The exercise consists of this: first, develop two or three "deserve" statements from your gratitude practice. Don't worry about the exact wording right now. It will clear itself up as you do the exercise. Make sure you have all the elements in each of the statements.

Then, each night for a minimum of two weeks, write out the statements ten times each. Do this for each statement every night for two weeks. It accomplishes a number of things on many different levels. Not many people are willing to sacrifice the hour of TV that it takes to write out the statements. Not many people are leading a blissful, growing life of plenty, either.

This is the first step in developing the will and the ability to focus it. It also works at a subconscious level on your beliefs about deserving and being "less than," and on improving your self-esteem. The proof is in the *doing*. You will never know the powerful effects of this exercise unless you do it.

We will continue to develop the will and our gratitude later. For now, continue doing your gratitude list in the morning and writing out the "deserve" statements at night. You will see fantastic differences if you do it with full effort.

In taking a quick look back at the Twelve Steps and at the programs that use them, you can see we have expanded the scope of work, and also the scope of accountability. We will discuss Grace later, but for now, it is apparent that we cannot cop out to being powerless and out of control. We cannot be passive in using our will. We must take responsibility for where we are and for changing it. The concept of being powerless in the Twelve Steps is being powerless in the face of our addiction. We have moved beyond that definition.

I decided to get and receive help that led to my getting sober. God supplied the grace, allowing me to see past my compulsion to make a decision, but it was my decision! I was not powerless! Just as I am not powerless on a daily basis to renew that decision not to drink today. I needed help, and, with grace, was able to accept it—but the *decision* was mine.

We cannot continue to take that away from people. It is the beginning of the power of invoking the will to change. For so many years, we gave up our ability to choose. We must affirm it when we do choose! It builds self-esteem and the ability to continue to grow and change. I made the decision, and I stopped drinking and drugging.

In the same way, I have made the choices to continue to grow and expand spiritually. The program gave me some tools. When those tools became less effective, I moved on to continue to grow, by choice, because I had the ability and the power to use my will to make decisions.

If we say that it is God's will and not ours, then we are limited by our understanding of God's will and the opportunities presented to carry that out. It is the same as being a victim of circumstance and chance. The responsibility passes from us.

However, God's greatest gift is free will. We can choose! Therefore, we are accountable for where we are and what we are becoming. Many people in the program "surrender," and become just as addicted to meetings as they were to drink, drugs, food, sex, and so on. They trade one compulsion for another.

It is our choice to be more, give more, have more, become more. We choose to grow, and to accept accountability for that choice. We pray in thanksgiving for the ability to choose. We pray in thanksgiving for the lessons received from good choices and not-so-good choices. We pray in thanksgiving for the power of grace that allows choices when we may be incapacitated from addiction.

The will is our greatest tool for becoming. Gratitude points out the lessons and direction. Will gives us the ability to move, opening all the possibilities and potentials to us. We are not limited. We can move beyond our perception and understanding through choice. We can grow and expand. The universe is ours.

We will return to the will when we discuss purpose, in the context of the Eleventh Step and how *choosing* to align ourselves with God's will brings power and grace actively into our lives. It is through the choice of purpose that we make this happen.

Right now let's discuss some of the things which block the use of the will, and some other issues that get in the way of gratitude. We will also discuss forgiveness in regard to those issues, so we may release them and stop the blockage of love.

Forgiveness

For if you forgive other people their failures,
your Heavenly Father will also forgive you.
—Gospel of Matthew 6.14

Forgiveness and self-forgiveness are two of the biggest areas many neglect in Twelve Step programs. The issue of amends is addressed, but usually not in the context of forgiveness. Forgiveness, as we will be discussing it, is an act of cancelling those thoughts, feelings, resentments, and so on that stand in the way of our loving another or ourselves.

Forgiveness is actively removing the blocks to unconditional love of self, another, or God—removing the conditions, demands, and expectations we've held that have not been met and therefore stop the flow of our love. Cancelling is not forgetting. It is not absolving the person from the act which caused us pain, anger, frustration, or humiliation. It is cancelling the demand, condition, or expectation that another person be or do anything different to receive our love.

We are not our actions. I may act in a "bad" way, but that does not mean I am "bad." My actions are separate from my being. I may act poorly, and I am responsible for that act. I may act nobly, and I am responsible for *that* act. But neither act is an indication that I am "poor" or "noble." It just means that I am capable of both poor and noble acts. I am responsible for those actions, and the same holds for others.

Forgiveness moves beyond the act to the person, and restores our love. It is very much like the story of Buddha talking about anger. Buddha said that anger is like a hot burning coal, that when I pick it up to throw it at you, *my* hand gets burned. By holding onto our anger, hurt, disappointment, frustration, and resentment, we get hurt by it. Our bodies, emotions, and minds get "burned" by not letting go, by not forgiving.

Edith Stauffer, Ph.D., in her book *Unconditional Love and Forgiveness*, gives excellent material and details great exercises for forgiveness. In *The Next Step Workbook*, I go over those exercises and others. It is well worth your while to look at both books. I am only going to give a couple of the simpler exercises here to start the forgiving process.

It is only necessary to realize that we are the ones being hurt from lack of forgiveness, not the person whom we need to forgive. Our holding back harms us, not them.

To start the process, a very simple list is done every morning, along with the blessings list. The new list is of all those hurts, resentments, frustrations, and angers that you remember, going as far back as possible. I discovered in doing movement therapy that the body holds these experiences and "incorporates" them. Then over the years we buffer ourselves from them through stiffness, unnatural posture, fat, restricted movement, and so on. When we release these experiences it is like a weight being released.

So, my list might be something like this:

Terry sitting on my chest in kindergarten and making me cry	I can let that go
Candi pulling a knife on me for teasing and scaring me	I can let that go
Peeing on Mrs. Faulkner's rug	I can let that go
Val hitting me when I was 7	I can let that go
Carol turning me down for a date at 15	I can let that go

and so on.

At first, some people experience an intensifying of the incident by writing it down on a list, but after a week or so, the charge on it lessens, then drops. This exercise allows us to bring to a conscious level hurts and injuries that at a younger age we didn't cope with well, and release them now, as we recognize them. We don't have to protect the younger us any more, by buffering with fat, or disappearing through thinness, or becoming stiff and unmovable, or deadening the feelings with alcohol, drugs, food, sex, and so forth.

We let go of lingering feelings of hurt, anger, and suffering that we've "held" in our bodies for a long time. As we progress with our list, a strange thing starts to occur. Rather than being concerned with the actions of others, we focus on our own feelings as we get more current. It becomes apparent that it is not the action of another that causes us pain, but rather our *reaction* to it. As we become aware of this, we see the patterns in our holding and the feelings we hold against ourselves which are causing all kinds of illness, "dis-ease," rigidity, and stiffness. As your list progresses into the third week, it might look something like this:

Being critical and judgmental of my wife	I can let that go
Being afraid of success at writing	I can let that go
Being afraid of failure at writing	I can let that go
Having doubt about my worthiness to teach	I can let that go
Being critical and negative to my children	I can let that go
Exaggerating to Tom about work	I can let that go

and so on.

So, in addition to naming the feeling or event that hurts, injures, or causes resentment, we make a statement of release. It is very important to do this daily. Unlike a daily 10th Step inventory, this is a list of feelings and concerns. It is not about making amends, but about self-forgiveness and acceptance. We release judgements, demands, conditions, and expectations of ourselves and others, and move on. We release and grow.

For deeper forgiveness issues, I recommend *The Next Step Workbook* or Edith Stauffer's book *Unconditional Love and Forgiveness*. For now, we will discuss the main venue for growth and awareness we all experience: relationships.

Relationships

*But let there be spaces in your togetherness,
and let the winds of the heavens dance
between you. Love one another, but make
not a bond of love. Let it rather be a moving
sea between the shores of your souls.*
—*Kahlil Gibran*

In a very real sense, being concerned about relationships is wasted energy. We are already established in a perfect relationship. We just don't know it. Our relationship with God, which is the model for all relationships, is perfect. We are established in the flow, as an awareness of connection and unity, through gratitude, and are one with our Higher Power. If we are not aware of it, it doesn't mean it doesn't exist. It does!

Relationships with other people, especially spouses or significant others, reflect that awareness. We connect with a piece of God in the other person. We sense the presence of the flow in them and react to it. The more established we are in our practice of gratitude and awareness, the more open we are to sensing the flow in others. There is no separation. We are all one—distinct pieces in this form, but all one.

In marriages or primary relationships, we tend to forget, or lose awareness of being connected. We confuse lust, loyalty, infatuation, affection, etc. for love. Then, when the lust goes away and the affection dies, we think we have "fallen out of love." Love is the awareness of being whole, each of us part of the whole, the flow. Seeing that connection and being it is beyond lust and affection, beyond addiction and compulsion. It *is*.

When we open to that awareness, we have tremendous relationships where we nurture and support each other in our growth and expansion. When we don't, we get caught up in separateness and differences. We blame and judge. We protect ourselves from pain and abandonment, when it is our lack of awareness that creates distance and separation.

Relationships are the opportunity to see the gift of choice put into action, to choose to love and open to the experience of wholeness, or to choose to see separateness and difference.

God's gift of will gives us the ability to grow and expand immeasurably in the forum of relationships. Relationships are where growth is measured and tested. It is where we face the rough mirror of ourselves in another and see the gifts received. It is an incredible arena for growth.

Many people complain about hard relationships and the amount of work necessary to maintain them. We should rejoice in the hard ones! That is where the gifts and lessons are. Easy ones teach us very little. We will briefly talk about other types of relationships, but the main focus will be on primary ones: man-wife, significant other. That is where we face the intensity, passion, holding, and big feelings which affect all areas of our lives.

The main topic we'll approach has big implications in every area of our life. This topic is **resistance**. What, exactly, is resistance? It is any thing or person that causes delay, friction, defense, fear, questioning, refusal, denial, doubt, anger, criticism, or withholding of the way we want to do things. Resistance is not getting our way, for whatever reason. Usually, we point a finger outward when faced with resistance. We like to blame, especially in relationships, but resistance is there for a very specific purpose.

Resistance is God's gift to us for becoming. It is the forge and furnace melding our focus and growth. It is the fine stone against which we sharpen our edge. Without resistance, we would lack resolve, character, and strength. Resistance is the teacher—the testing of the mettle. It is grand stuff.

Of course, it doesn't seem like it. When we are in the middle of an argument, for the thousandth time, about money, it is hard to see resistance as a force for our benefit, but it is. When I am in the middle of explaining my new approach to becoming healthy and slim, and my wife laughs out loud instead of giving me support, it is hard to see the good in that. When we are caught in the emotion or addiction of the moment, it is hard to see outside of it to discover the benefit.

Gratitude allows us to gain that perspective. By seeing the gift in the moment, it allows us to detach from the emotion and see the resistance for what it is—an arrow pointing in the direction of our growth, saying, "Look! Here it is! Your next lesson!" However, it is very difficult to see things that way at first. It takes the practice of gratitude.

Resistance shows in all we do that is not in line with our purpose and will. Even then, the greatest resistance and testing may occur in resisting our noble purpose. It gives us a force to grow against. Like Hercules lifting the growing calf every day, our growing against increasing resistance gives strength and resolve. Without resistance, we have no way to grow.

A lot of what happens in relationships is **projection**. Projection is throwing back at the other person those things or issues which are our own problems. It can take many forms. "You never pay any attention to me. You always have something else on your mind. It is always 'me' with you. Can't you give me some of your time?"

We complain about what we are unable to give. If we find ourselves complaining and blaming, it makes sense to check first to see if we are projecting. Become accountable! The good thing about resistance is that it allows us to see those areas *we* have problems with. It throws back in our faces the areas where *we* can grow. It is the perfect teacher.

The ultimate resistance is in being accountable for how we feel. It is so easy to blame our feelings on other people, circumstances, or situations. When we are unhappy, it is easy to blame our spouses for "making" us unhappy: "If she would only pay more attention to me. If she would only earn more money at her job to take the pressure off me financially. If only ..."

We make how we feel conditional. We'll be happy, *if only*. So we have expectations, demands, and conditions that have to be met in order to feel a certain way. It is very insidious and subtle. We blame the other person, usually the one closest to us, for how we feel. Ken Keyes, Jr. , in his books, calls this addictive programming, to be addicted to a certain type of behavior or thoughts of another. We make them responsible for our emotions. We give up our power, and leave how we feel up to chance and circumstance, since we can't control the other person. We also place a tremendous burden on them, which they grow to resent.

We must take responsibility for how we feel, if we are to have satisfactory and fulfilling relationships. It is not what someone else does or doesn't do that makes us feel a certain way. It is how we *choose* to see it! It is our perspective of what is happening that determines our feelings, not the action itself. That is very hard to accept.

Spiritual growth is measured by the amount of accountability a person takes for their inner life. Becoming accountable for the way *you* feel is a big step in that direction. Gaining perspective and detachment comes from the practice of gratitude. Being accountable is an act of our will. It is a choice!

Of course, we are affected by the actions of others, and the closer they are to us, the more we will be affected, but it is important to realize that we choose how we are affected. I am responsible for the way I feel. I choose to be happy. The actions of my lover don't make me happy or unhappy. They may affect the quality of my happiness—quite often they do, but my choice is to be happy.

This can get pretty confusing, especially when we are going through a rough emotional time. Divorce, separation, and other highly emotional times tend to bring out the blamer in us. If only the other person would act this way or do that, we would feel better. "They" made me feel this miserable! We give our power of choice over to the other person, and let them dictate how we feel. It is frustrating and humiliating when this happens, yet how often do we let it happen? Sure, we are affected by the actions of another, but our feelings are our *own!*

The stronger we get spiritually, the more we can open to emotional situations and be a humble, vulnerable mirror for the feelings of the other person involved. The stronger we are, the more gentle we can be in any situation. By surrendering to the flow of emotions, we can let them wash over and through us, and when they are gone, we still remain, happy, secure, and established in the flow of God's love and grace.

Learning to be unconditional in our relationships, with no expectations, demands, or conditions, is the key to becoming more open, available, loving, and forgiving.

My first marriage ended after 11 years while I was still drinking. It should have ended. My wife endured much more and much longer than she should have. Seeing the good in that situation was seeing the good in ending it. Not that there weren't many lessons and gifts in the relationship, because there were, but the ending of it caused me eventually to seek help and to get sober.

My second marriage, a few years later, got off to a very shaky start. Although I had been sober almost three years when we got married, I still had many addictive and sick behaviors. Getting married again brought all those behaviors into focus, as they bounced off my mate. It soon was apparent that we needed help if the marriage was to last.

I would get angry and blame it on my wife. She wasn't doing *this* right, or she didn't do *that* right, or she didn't understand the pressures on a big shot like me. She also blamed how she felt on me. I caused her to feel miserable and upset. I caused her to feel insecure and withdrawn.

We went to a counselor who, after one session, decided I was the one he needed to see, and that my wife needn't return. I was appalled. I was sure she was the cause of much of the trouble in our relationship, and that if she would get help, a lot would be resolved. The therapist assured me that because of my better-developed sense of self, we would be able to make more progress with me than with my wife. Boy, was I suckered!

So I started seeing Ed once a week. We started out discussing the relationship and my sobriety, and soon Ed told me that we would work on my anger and the Third Step. I didn't think my anger was very out of hand; in fact, I didn't think I had much anger at all. To work on the Third Step was a spiritual practice, not a proper focus for a therapist, I thought. Ed asked me to try it for a while and see what resulted, so I did.

Ed asked me to start reading about meditation. He had me keep a dream journal. We discussed my family and experiences. It soon became apparent that I projected a lot of my problems on my wife. I accused her of rigidity and unwillingness to see my side of things. Just the opposite was true. I was rigid and unyielding. I accused her of withholding and rejection. I was the rejecter.

And my anger became open! I was angry about my childhood. I was angry about my first marriage, my disease, my life, and I vented my anger in many ways by directing it towards my wife.

Ed and I worked together for almost two years while I learned detachment, release, openness of expression, and spiritual pursuits. It was a painful, stimulating growth experience. Without the *resistance* of my wife, I never would have been pushed into growing, and I never would have started the next level of my spiritual path.

I left Ed when we reached the limits of what he could teach me and what I could give in return, and I found a new mentor. My new teacher, Michael, took me even further into spiritual growth through Raja Yoga and the practice of breathing, meditation, and concentration exercises. My meditation deepened. My detachment and singled-pointed concentration improved. My joy and serenity increased. My marriage ended.

In the growth, my wife and I discovered we were moving in different directions. We also discovered that we had different levels of commitment and trust. We assumed we were through with each other.

We both moved on to other relationships. We kept in contact, and were aware of each other's progress, but for almost two years we stayed out of each other's way. Then we each discovered that we were still dealing with a few of the same issues that had plagued us together, and we decided to use our relationship with each other as the forum to learn these lessons and to help each other grow.

We did a marathon weekend together to work out the parameters of trust and respect we had for each other. We decided to try to let the past be the past, and stay in the now. We moved to new levels of communication. At the same time, my awareness of gratitude was maturing and we practiced that together. We became a source of teaching and inspiration to each other. Part of the teaching was that although we loved each other, we were not meant to spend our lives together. After learning the lessons on trust and grace from each other, we would move on to new and different lessons. It was a hard thing to accept, yet at an intuitive level, we knew that to grow more we needed to let go.

We will always be connected, and use each other to test lessons and gifts for validity and ego-attachment, but we will move faster and further being apart. It has not been easy. It has brought up many areas that still need work.

Without gratitude and resistance, I never would have been given this gift! It is not easy. It has taken years of work and focus to move beyond my beliefs, knowledge, and learning to that place of experiencing the flow of creation, plenty, and glory that is God's gift of connection. It can happen to all of us, with commitment through the use of will to action and gratitude.

Relationships give us the place to work, to give and receive the gifts and lessons, to test and expand, to open and accept. Being totally strong gives us the ability to be totally vulnerable. The ultimate gift in relationships is vulnerability. Most of us spend years learning to hide our vulnerability and to move away from the pain.

Yet the pain is the pointer to our area of growth. Strong emotion is the beacon, signalling the presence of the gift. We are so lucky to be given the ability to use emotion as the language of gratitude. What an awesome gift! What an awesome challenge, to be able to detach from the emotion enough to see the gift in it. Emotion is a terrific present to use for our benefit.

By using the will to choose how a relationship can help every one involved, the gifts and lessons become apparent. What we choose to do with them is also a challenge, but we have the choice.

Occasionally we are in relationships where we don't see the choice, where we feel dead-ended with no way out.

When we were children, our relationship with our parents could be a very scary and confusing place to be. Much has been written about the ACOA movement and the tremendous confusion and turmoil of growing up in an alcoholic household. Any dysfunctional situation can cause great problems, not the least of which is no "normal" modeling of what constitutes a good relationship.

If we are in an abusive relationship, either as a child with an abusive parent, or later in life, it seems that much of the time there is no choice. Besides the confusion and pain of the abuse from someone who "loves" us, there is the guilt of thinking we caused it and deserve it—and sometimes the secret enjoyment of it. It is a very difficult situation, and I am not an expert.

But I do know this. Having survived being emotionally, physically, and sexually abused as a child, growing up and becoming an alcoholic, getting sober, and continuing to grow spiritually, I was given insight through gratitude. Part of the insight I was given confused and disquieted me until I was able to absorb it, because, you see, the experience of the flow from God that comes through gratitude is from a place of much higher wisdom. My Higher Self can see beyond my knowledge, experience, and belief, and my insights contain that higher wisdom.

Part of the insight I received let me acknowledge that the gift of comfort I provided in being abused was more important to my abuser than the pain was to me. I know this is hard to understand, as I have struggled with it for some time. It became apparent to me that the cold comfort I received from my mother was not for my benefit—it was for hers. And the touch and affection given by my abusive father was for his benefit, not mine. I chose where and how, as a child, I would deal with those problems. I was strong and different, even then. Looking back, I can see how I separated, survived, and grew.

I don't know if every abused child has these thoughts and awareness later in life. I suspect not. I know that my brothers and sisters have endured a terrible adjustment over the years to their childhood experiences and are still dealing with problems associated with our family life.

My family is a perfect example of the futility of trying to move into relationships while ignoring the lessons and gifts offered in them. My oldest brother is an alcoholic and may be one of the unhappiest people I know. Both my sisters have had multiple marriages, as have I. My younger brothers are also alcoholics, one practicing and one not, and one of my younger brothers has a couple of marriages under his belt. We all seem to continue to mirror the way we were raised.

Thus we carry forward the legacy of relationships. Until we open to the gifts and lessons offered, and move on to the next levels of honesty, openness, acceptance, and growth, we are doomed to be faced with the same conditions and situations, over and over. Only when we look for the good, be that what it may—even if it is leaving the situation—and accept the lesson, will we be able to move on to the next lesson.

Ask God for the will and gratitude to accept and see a relationship for what it is. Then look for the good. See the lesson or gift offered, and be grateful for it.

Gratitude gives us the ability to stay current in relationships. If we are grateful, moment to moment, then we are not keeping the pains of the past alive, nor are we borrowing trouble from the future. We are in the infinity of the now, with all the gifts God has offered. Is it easy? No! But with practice it gets easier and easier, and soon we become established in the now and grateful for it all.

We will come back to relationships in other contexts as we explore more issues of growth. It is important to keep all of what we practice and learn in the focus of relationships, because we are related. All of us. To become a monk or nun or spiritual hermit, and move into a cave in the mountains, only avoids the real issues. What is harder and contains the greater gift: maintaining silence or speaking only with grace and truth, and only when it will help others? What is the greater lesson: being strictly vegetarian and fasting, or eating in health and balance and accepting the gifts of lovingly prepared food from others, in moderation? Which is more of a gift: being able to focus and grow toward God in solitude, or being able to focus and give the gift of growing toward God in society?

Spiritual growth means little unless it benefits others and is apparent in everyday life. We will next discuss a major area of resistance, **prosperity**, and then put growth into action!

Prosperity

The whole world of loneliness, poverty, and pain make a mockery of what human life should be.

—Bertrand Russell

Prosperity is one of the major issues of resistance, in a relationship or by ourselves. It is a major indicator of our position about deserving, which we discussed earlier, and is a good outside measure of self-esteem.

Prosperity (or success) to most people is measured by money. We will be discussing success in terms of lifestyle later, but for right now we will discuss money. Money is the cause of more friction and resistance in marriage (89% of marriages that end in divorce have money as one of the root issues, according to the American Bar Association), relationships, business relationships, and our relationship with ourselves than any other issue. We all seem to have a lot of confusion over money. Spiritually, we are taught that *the love of* money is the root of all evil. In society we are taught that money is the measure of success and status. Those of us raised by parents who went through the Depression or whose grandparents went through the Depression have been given lessons on **lack**: that there is never enough, and one must make do with what one has.

In advertising and the media, we are given lessons all the time about what we "need" to have in order to be successful, sexually attractive, powerful, and special. No wonder we are confused and ambiguous in our attitudes toward money, prosperity, and success! Let's see if we can clear the air about how these things fit into a spiritual path.

Money in and of itself is neutral, neither evil nor good. It is *how we use money* and *what we think of money* that give it meaning. Churches, missions, bibles, salaries of priests, ministers, nuns, schools, hospitals, and so on all cost money—a lot of money. Earning money to be used for these purposes and many more cannot be considered bad or evil. The more money one earns, the more one is able to contribute for these purposes. How can that be construed in any way but good? Yet we get mixed messages from "religious" and "spiritual" teachers about having a lot of money. It is considered somehow less spiritual to be rich, as if having money and being able to contribute more to the necessities of running a church or spiritual organization lowers a person on the spiritual path.

We are given the impression that there is a limited amount of money available, and that by being rich we are depriving someone else of their fair share. Somehow, through the Depression mentality mainly, we've learned that there is a limited supply of everything! We are taught this poverty consciousness, that there is not enough money, time, road, opportunity, oil, education, pretty ladies, or handsome men.

We are taught in the media that the "good things" in life are limited, so we better grab our share while we can. Go for the gusto and the heck with the other guy. Hold on tight to what we've got, because there is always someone wanting to take it away. Go for all we can get, because there is a limited supply, and if we don't get it, the next guy will.

The reality of the situation is that we live in an unlimited universe. God's gifts are ever expanding, and there is more than enough for everybody. Granted, we have limited resources on this planet and are making a mess of our environment, but that actually provides more! More opportunity to find solutions, for creative people to step forward to help others, for profit to those who can provide helpful service. There is unlimited opportunity! There is an unlimited range of services that can be given and expanded. There is an unlimited scope of creativity. It is absolutely mind-boggling to become aware of the expanse and flow of the universe and all that is available to us.

It has been said that if all the money in the world were collected, then divided up equally among all people, within a year it would all be back in the same hands! In other words, we all have what we deserve—what a concept! That is the problem facing most people: we don't have a realistic concept of how to become *worth* more, and we haven't cleared our confusion about *deserving* more.

We are so limited in our thinking that we concentrate on the lack rather than on the opportunity. We are reinforced in that kind of thinking by everything around us. The power and directness of purpose opens our awareness to opportunity. With gratitude, we begin to see the good in any situation, and can move past the lack. Perspective is the difference between a rich man and a poor man. The rich man sees the opportunity, the poor man sees the lack, and of course, the rich man sees that he deserves it.

We will be talking about balance in lifestyle and attitude later, but for now let's assume that all things are equal except perspective between the rich man and the poor one. It is how we see the world that determines whether we see limits or opportunity, and it is a choice. We can choose to see it differently, if our view of things is holding us back. How we see things is a function of our purpose and the goals we set to implement that purpose.

It is important to keep in mind that goals need to be in line with our overall purpose in order to be powerful and compelling. Goals are the short-term and long-term filters we place on our output of mind which direct our actions. Goals give impetus and direction for discipline. It is important to realize that goals are specific tools to use for growth. We'll talk later about setting goals in terms of purpose, to give us a different perspective on how we reach goals.

A goal is important for who we have to become in order to reach that goal, not for the goal itself. In other words, when we set a goal it is important to remember who we will become in reaching it. If you want to become a millionaire, it is being a millionaire that is important, not the million dollars. Let me explain. You can win a lottery for a million dollars, and if you are not a millionaire, it will not take long before that million dollars is gone. If, on the other hand, you *are* a millionaire, but broke, it will not take long to get a million dollars, if you choose.

I read of a study done in New York of the first 40 lottery winners who won a million dollars or more. In taking a look at their lives a few years after their winning, the study found that most of the winners were broke, in trouble with alcohol or drugs, had family problems, and were basically unhappy. They were not millionaires, and they did not keep their millions. In a reunion of lottery winners in Washington state, the same thing was apparent. Money did not solve their problems. If anything, it exaggerated them.

If we want more in life, we must become more. We must expand, if our life is to expand. Our goals must stretch and enlarge us, if we are to get more from life. How much more valuable must we become in order to be a millionaire, if that is our goal? How much better at managing time, being creative, managing money? How much better at people skills? It is a question of value that determines how much we get out of life.

If money is the measure of our success, then we must expand our value in order to create more money in our life.

If you are earning $15 an hour and working forty hours a week and you want to earn more money, you have a couple of choices. You can work more hours or you can make yourself more valuable than $15 dollars an hour. If you are limited in the hours you can work, whether by your employer or circumstances at work, or by choice in wanting time for other pursuits, then you must make your time more valuable. Assuming you are putting full effort into your time for $15 an hour, how do you become more valuable?

You can't work harder or more hours. So, you must grow! You must become capable of putting more value into the hour. It is not a matter of working harder. It is a matter of becoming more. So, it is outside the job that you must expand. You must become more as a person, maybe by taking classes in some area of work, but more likely by taking classes in some area of expansion as a person, perhaps public speaking or sports. Take classes that expand your ability to communicate: again, public speaking, English, writing, or psychology. Perhaps try books, seminars, or tapes that cause you to expand and grow.

It becomes fairly obvious to one who examines it: standard education gets standard results. Exceptional education gets exceptional results. We must give ourselves an exceptional education in order to expand and become more valuable. This education can be reached in many different ways—experience, classes, seminars, tapes, books, mentors, etc.—but it must be done in order to grow, and we must grow in order to be worth more. What, exactly, does it mean to be worth more or have more value?

It means being able to provide more or better service. Our goal, in becoming more, needs to incorporate the ability to give and share more. That is how we expand and grow spiritually and financially. They are not mutually exclusive. The same universal principles apply. Give more and we receive more. The laws of compensation that Napoleon Hill wrote about in *Think and Grow Rich* are constant. Sow and you shall reap! Always, but the sowing must come first. The better we become at sowing, the larger will be our harvest.

So, prosperity is a matter of becoming aware we deserve the bounty of the universe. We do this through the practice of will and by realizing that we are unlimited children of God, with equal opportunity and challenge. Then we take a look at the unlimited nature of opportunity. Those who see lack are *trained* to see it, and we can train ourselves to see opportunity through the practice of gratitude. We can expand and grow by becoming more and giving more. The universe and God respond by giving us more.

There is a flip side to the issue of success, money, and prosperity. That side has to do with how we spend our money, our time, and other resources, and it also has to do with greed. Most people see greed in a very limited sense, but greed can be pervasive and very detrimental. Greed is the process of grasping and holding onto something while the opportunity to expand is passing by. It is pulling out of the process of expansion in order to *keep* something. It is lessening the value of something, without realizing that it reduces our value at the same time.

When you buy something, you never pay retail. You always look for the discount. It is a crime to pay full price, when you can pay less. Do you know someone like that? I used to think that way, until I realized what it was saying about myself and others. First, it is saying that I think that my supply of money is limited, so I need to stretch it as far as possible by paying as little as possible for everything. Second, it is saying that I don't think I'm worth paying full value for quality. Since my resources are limited, I better settle for less. Third, it is saying that the value of the other persons' goods or service is not as valuable as priced. So, the overall effect is to grasp what I've got and maintain limited thinking, rather than casting my resources into the flow to multiply and expand. It is saying that I am not worth the best, and that

I don't shop where the best is offered. It is contracting and limiting, and it is insidious.

The same can be said about those who don't tip in large percentages or who are always looking for the free alternative to paying for convenience. I am not suggesting extravagance. I am suggesting moving past limited thinking and letting the universe expand for us.

There is another side to this, those people who are in business for themselves and try to determine fair pricing for goods and services when they have not resolved the issue of money, success, and prosperity in their own mind. Most of the time, a person with a mentality of lack will underprice their goods and services, thinking it is of little value because they don't see the value in themselves. Or if there is greed (which is the mirror of lack) in operation, then the goods or service may end up overpriced. Either way limits the flow of resources in the universe.

A fair price is that based on what value a thing or service has in an unlimited universe. A person cannot base price on need. We do a disservice to someone if we discount a price, as it reflects a lower value of our service and it reflects on the self-value of the person we discount for. In a workshop or class situation, a scholarship or trade can be arranged for a limited number of folks who can't afford it otherwise, but it must be of equal value or more.

Moving in an unlimited universe, as a deserving child of God, I pay full value for services and goods provided, looking always for quality, as I am a quality person and deserve the best. The services and goods I provide are of the highest quality, as they reflect who I am, and I price them fairly based on their value. In so doing, I keep the flow of value increasing as I become more valuable, and am able to give more value as the flow increases. It is a wonderful cycle. It is fulfilling and unlimited.

It is in determining value that we reflect our self-esteem and our attitude of prosperity. Value is a relative thing, usually based on how a person thinks of self and how much they project their value onto the objects and services they buy. People who are insecure, if they have a lot of money, are willing to pay extraordinary sums for goods or services in order to prove their worth as a person: getting their hair done at the "in" salon, buying furs and jewelry at super high prices, having the "right" car or house in the "right" neighborhood.

We are just stewards. God owns it all! We have the use of things for a short time, sometimes we can pass them on to others, and then we are gone. God abides. Stewardship is the approach that makes the best sense, then. We are caretakers of the bounty God provides. The better caretakers we are, the more will be given to our care. The more we share and serve, the more God provides for us to share and steward. It makes so much sense when viewed this way. We can't own it. We just take care of it for awhile, and share what we can. God provides and expands based on our stewardship and the amount of sowing we do. It is like the tides—inevitable!

Ultimately, if we determine our purpose (which we discuss later) and surrender into it, we will be doing something we love for a living, the value will be tremendous, and we will bathe in the prosperity of the universe. The universe cannot help but pay for value received. If we give, through our purpose, unlimited value, then we will receive unlimited reward in return. It is absolutely guaranteed. Sow and you will reap.

The hallmark of a truly liberated person in relation to money and success is **generosity**. Freedom is achieved through generosity. Being able to let go freely, and give to the universe as it gives to us—that is where realization of the flow is hidden.

I have always had the knack for making money, sometimes very good money, but I never was able to hold onto any of it and I never seemed to have any to give away. Then I got involved with a growth group. Part of what we decided to do was read *The Richest Man In Babylon* by George S. Clason. It was the second time I had gone through the book and I got a lot out of it. In our group, we decided to do a balance sheet and a monthly budget. I had heard all my life about the benefits of a budget, but I had never done a personal one. I decided, what the heck, I'm going for it, and I prepared a monthly budget and stuck to it. The first item on my budget was that 10% of my net, after taxes, went in savings. The second item on my budget was that 10% of my net, after taxes, I gave away. (Currently, I give it to my local food bank.) What a huge difference it made in my life immediately!

It is incredibly important to develop these habits of saving and tithing! It makes a tremendous difference in how we feel about money, and how the universe responds to us with money. I started my budget when I was not making much. In fact, it was a very big stretch to put money in savings and give it away. Within a very short period of time, I was making *much* more money and was able to save more and give more away. If we don't develop the habit now, how will we be able to give away 10% and save 10% when we are making big bucks? The Bible says, "Be faithful over small things, and I will make you master of many."

A commitment to being generous expands us as a person. It pushes us into bigger capability, and the money becomes just another instrument of the flow. Time is also a commodity of great value. Be generous with your time! It will expand also. Give your time to a worthy cause and you will be amazed at the payback.

Becoming prosperous means more than just money. It is a lifestyle and an attitude. Through the practice of gratitude, we can maintain balance and move forward spiritually while using prosperity as another instrument of growth. It is a matter of using the will to decide to change. It can happen. As we get in line with our purpose, prosperity just flows into our life.

Move into unlimited thinking! Let go of lack! Let go of poverty! Move into your rightful place as an unlimited child of God!

Action

No energy is lost in the world, nor is it merely the souls of men that are immortal but all their actions as well. They live on through their effects.

—*Goethe*

In any recovery program or growth program, action is the test of self. Have I changed? Can people tell by my *actions* that I am different? Have I put my intention and belief into action?

Growth comes from action. It is not only a matter of understanding or knowledge. It is not only a matter of learning or belief. It is *doing*. Meaning comes from the act. Thank God for the ability to choose and take action. Without it we would be stuck.

In *The Next Step Workbook*, I talk about two main actions that give us growth. To be in line with our sense of purpose and to move toward God, we must do at least these two things. First, we must use the will to choose and decide. We must invoke the power of the will to move toward growth and God. Second, we must share. *We must give away what we've gained in order to have room for more.* To expand and grow, we must give to others.

We've already discussed the will and the magnificent gift we've received. We've only touched on sharing a little. The Twelfth Step of the program talks about **sharing**. It is of paramount importance. It is how we become more, have more, and give more. It is not just the program we must share. It is all of it. Everything we've been given must be shared openly.

A spiritual awakening is the result of working the Twelve Steps, according to the program. Yet there are countless members of all the groups who are just as mired down in their problems as they've always been, in spite of working the Steps. Don't you think a spiritual awakening would make a difference in how a person lived, and in how problems and challenges would be handled? Of course it would. Once a person is sober, abstaining, or clean, it makes sense to move on to something that will make immediate differences in helping other areas of life as quickly as possible.

One example is the incredible power of influence. We are influenced every day, all day, by TV, radio, print media, and the people we associate with. We can make great differences in our life right away by limiting our exposure to negative influences.

Who am I around? What are they doing to me? Is it okay? The power of influence from those people we spend time with cannot be underestimated. It is subtle and important. Are we spending most of our time with negative people? Are we spending time with sick people? Where do we spend most of our time?

Some of where we spend our time can't be controlled, but most of it can be. I suggest to you that if you want to grow and expand, you need to spend time with people who are growing and expanding. Stick with the winners! Of course, we need to share and give to others, but the people who can use our sharing and giving are not necessarily the ones who need it. The people who can use our sharing and giving are the ones who will *use* it!

Look very carefully at the time you spend in meetings with recovering folks. Look very carefully at the time spent at coffee and other discussions with disturbed and sick people. Look very carefully at the time spent with people who can nurture your growth and help you expand and become. I would be willing to bet that those of you who are stuck spend much more time with negative, sick, disturbed folks, than with those who are expanding and growing and becoming. If that is so, what is it doing to you?

The universe operates on a "deserve" principle, not a "need" principle. All spiritual practices have laws of compensation such as: We shall reap what we have sown. What goes around, comes around. The Law of Karma. God is neutral in dispensing the magnificence of the universe. It is those who have sown who reap, not those who need it most or those who are sickest, but those who have sown. Grace operates in the universe for those incapable of caring for themselves. We are not in that situation.

Our situation is this: if we do not have in our life those things, people, experiences, gifts, and abilities that we want, then we have not taken enough action and sown the seeds necessary to receive them. Sowing includes hanging around those folks who have learned how to sow.

It is a hard lesson to learn, but a necessary one. Action is the sowing, moving in the direction of God and growth, giving the experience to those who will and can use it, and continuing to choose to move and grow. A spiritual awakening comes from the doing, always.

Action is a discipline that is learned. It comes from doing the little things *every day* that move us closer to our purpose and goals. Doing "will" statements (see *The Next Step Workbook* and the section on will) and determining the steps necessary for the next six months to a year to reach our goals is a necessity. We must act now.

It is very easy to put it off until the kids are out of school. *As soon as* I'm out of debt, I'll start a savings and tithing program. *As soon as* my divorce is over, I'll start a spiritual program. *As soon as* I find a better job, I'll start a personal growth program. *As soon as* I find the perfect significant other, I'll spend time reading and praying and developing myself. *As soon as* I have some stability in my sobriety, I'll start working other steps. *As soon as.*

Action leads to awakening. It cannot be put off. *As soon as* never comes. Take little steps, but do it now! Start putting a dollar, or even a quarter, aside every day to start your savings program. Make your first check out every month to your favorite charity for 10% of your net. If you can't do it now, what makes you think you'll be able to when you're making more money (just as we talked about on prosperity)?

Start meditating and praying every morning, as soon as you've done your gratitude list. Grow and expand from the *doing!* Action is the help God needs to perform miracles. The material is there; it is in the labor that we assist our Higher Power in becoming the full miracle we can be. Do it! Don't just read about it, or think about it, or wait for understanding. Do it! Every day, a little bit at a time.

We are so conditioned to expect instant results and instant gratification, that anything that takes more than a day to complete is beyond most of our capabilities. We want it now! Spiritual growth doesn't happen in a day. Becoming more, giving more, having more doesn't happen in a day. We must do a little each day, and build on it in the next. The reward is in the doing and the becoming. It is a dual reward that is incredible. We get satisfaction and reward from developing and performing the small disciplines daily. Just the accomplishment makes us feel good, and the day-to-day building of results from the discipline also rewards us.

So what gets in the way of our taking action? For most of us it is **fear**. We will discuss fear in many different ways and look at some methods of moving through and past fear next.

Fear

*To fear love is to fear life, and those who fear
life are already three parts dead.*
— *Bertrand Russell*

Fear hinders all parts of life. It shows itself as lateness,
greed, procrastination, hesitancy, rigidity, aggressiveness,
anger, being "right," bias, prejudice, compulsiveness, obses-
siveness, negativity, judgment, grasping, jealousy, defen-
siveness, caretaking—the list is endless. We disguise fear in
many different forms in order to justify lack of action and
change.

In relationships, fear is the killer of emotion and growth.
It keeps us from openly expressing who and what we are and
from opening to change. It keeps us from gentleness and
acceptance. Fear closes the opportunity to expand into
another and stops the chance for intimacy. It is the little
worm of doubt that eats away at our serenity and ease in a
relationship. It speaks of being unworthy and "less than."
Fear, in its many forms, keeps us from being who we really
are; we conform and comply out of fear.

Napoleon Hill, in his books on thinking and growing rich,
has a great approach to fear. He points out that no matter our
beliefs, in this form, it is going to end. Sometime, sooner or

later, it's over. We die. We can't take it with us and, at least as far as we know, we don't get a second chance in these bodies. It is going to stop. This is not a rehearsal. So, what have we got to lose?

Looking ahead, and seeing that it has got to end, why not go for it all now? Why wait until it is too late? Tell the people in your life that you love them *now*! Take a chance *now*! Grow and change *now*! It is no mistake that people who have a near-death experience become different folks. Their perspective changes. They see "the big picture." A lot of fear leaves their lives. They live *now*!

We must take a look at what is holding us back from changing and see if it is fear. If it is, then get some help in overcoming it. Get around people who are growing and changing. Get around folks who take some risks. Try doing some little things that make you uncomfortable, but are no big deal. Take a look at what there is "out there" that means anything to you, and give yourself a chance to express appreciation for it. Open yourself to experience the grace and joy in life. This is not easy. Fear is our biggest hurdle in life. It takes desire and will to make these changes and to move ahead, but the rewards are spectacular.

Fear is overcome through discipline. We have already discussed discipline and how it is its own reward. One of the main reasons discipline feels so good, is that each time we practice a little discipline, we push past fear. We move in a new and positive direction. We shed the old skin and give ourselves room to grow. We gain confidence and surety in the knowledge of our ability to overcome fear.

Frank Herbert, in his science fiction classic *Dune*, had Paul (the hero in the book) use a litany against fear that was very effective. It was a discipline used to put fear in proper perspective and to release and use effectively the energy that fear creates. It is a very good reminder that we can *use* fear to help, and that the energy created is powerful and important. It can move us past the fear into action!

> *I must not fear. Fear is the mind-killer. Fear
> is the little-death that brings total obliteration.
> I will face my fear. I will permit it to pass over
> me and through me. And when it has gone
> past I will turn the inner eye to see its path.
> Where the fear has gone there will be nothing.
> Only I will remain.*
>
> —*Frank Herbert*

Let's take a look at some common fears.

Perhaps one of the main fears we have is that of being inferior, of not deserving, of being "less than." Included in this are fear of success and failure, fear of abandonment and commitment, fear of abundance and poverty. These fears are tied to our low self-esteem. All of us, in one way or another, suffer from damaged or low self-esteem. We compensate for it in many ways, some by overachieving to become deserving, and some by underachieving to prove our lack is deserved. We sabotage our lives to make sure we fit our self-image, which is usually warped and unconsciously low. We destroy relationships, work situations, friendships, and our relationship with God to make sure we don't challenge our perception of where we belong in the scheme of life.

Fear keeps us from seeing that we are children of God, created with equal opportunity to play in the vastness and plenty of the universe. We all get equal chances to suffer and enjoy. We all get equal opportunity to create and destroy. We all have the same gifts of pain and pleasure. We may have different talents and inclinations, but, we have the same opportunity to overcome problems and challenges and to take advantage of opportunities and lessons. Those who wish to expand and grow ask for more problems and challenges, for it is in the overcoming of the problems and challenges that we *become more!* In accepting the fear associated with moving into problems, we move past it. This allows us to give more and show others how to move past fear, which creates room for more in our lives.

Fear signals our opportunity to grow. It gives us the chance to move through it and co-create, with God, the new us, a bigger being, capable of giving and receiving more from life, who can move, in spite of fear, to be more, have more, give more. Fear is our opportunity to change our low self-esteem and grow into a deserving self-image, an unlimited child of God, capable and deserving, able to grow and expand. This is accomplished, not *without* fear, but *through* fear, a little step at a time, consistently challenging fear and moving anyway. We become a delightful child of a loving God, using the gifts provided to play in the unlimited universal playground of God.

We start to change our self-concept with simple "deserve" statements. (See *The Next Step Workbook* for specific exercises.) By working every night writing out our deserve statements, and developing perspective on our true relationship to our Higher Power, we come to understand our equal stature with all living beings. We all deserve the best. We all have been given the opportunity to find it and enjoy it, according to our own definitions and growth. We are not limited by someone else's idea of what is or isn't best for us. "Best" is our own idea of where we stand now, in relationship to God and the universe, based on our growth and understanding now. That idea changes and expands as we grow.

All it takes is the practice of simple disciplines today and every day. The main fear we all have is really a fear of separation from God. We feel, and project, our separation from the flow, and it becomes our fear of being separated "out there" from the things we have chosen to make important. We fear separation from our loved ones, abandonment, success, failure, and so on, all of which, at their base, are fears of separation and lack of relationship with God. When we realize that we are never separated, and never have been, we lose fear. This is not something that happens at an intellectual or emotional level. Loss of fear happens as an acknowledgement of experience that has always been, and always will be, part of and in the flow of creation with God.

Moving past fear comes from the awakening that happens from doing—not understanding, or learning, or knowing, or believing, but from *doing*! Loss of fear comes from practice of gratitude, prayer, meditation, deserve statements, and will statements, on a daily basis. These are little disciplines which, done daily without fail, build on themselves and create new results.

Another fear that seems to be common is the fear of losing control of what is happening around us or of not being able to control ourselves; of being manipulated and persuaded against our will; of choosing something or someone "bad" for us. Control is a big issue with most people, especially addictive and codependent people.

Let's take a closer look at control. What, exactly, is it? For most of us, it is being able to maintain a certain predictability of a situation and know with reasonable certitude the outcome of any action. It also means being able to manipulate or manage any gathering of people or one-on-one situation to our advantage and to what we see as best for the others. Control means being in charge, directing the action and knowing the outcome.

How often are we really in control of anything? Of course, God's gift of the will gives us control of ourselves (except when we are ill or disabled). We can choose what we will do and say and decide. But other than ourselves, do we have any control? Of course not. Other folks are also operating from free will, even as children—maybe *especially* as children. We can suggest and teach and persuade, but we cannot choose for another, so fear of losing control is really an illusion. We cannot lose control of ourselves, except through intoxication or incapacity, and we have no control over others, so the fear is baseless.

Yet it is a valid fear. It signals our lack of faith in our will, and our unwillingness to accept the great gift God has given us. It is a paradox. To fear lack of control means we think we can't make our own choices, yet the fear itself keeps us from accepting the fact that we can choose. It is not seeing the nature of control for what it is that causes us trouble. When we speak of control, we are really speaking of control of others and the situation, and that is something we can never control, as we are a part of it, not the director.

Doing will exercises daily allows us to move past this fear and to gain perspective on it. Doing irritation list exercises also allows us to let go of the anger, frustration, fear, and other self-inflicted anguishes of seeming lack of control. Controlling people are also quick to judge and negate, some of the traits I will to lessen in myself. Through daily gratitude and release exercises, I came to the full realization of my place in the universe and the fact that no control is needed except self-control through the practice of discipline. With the practice of gratitude, will, meditation, and prayer, we get stronger and gentler every day.

Earnie Larsen, in *Stage II Recovery*, talks about overcoming habits as the key to change. His book is a wonderful little guide to moving beyond the first part of recovery. He feels that fear is our unconscious fighting to maintain habit. He may be right. Habit is a choice, just like everything else in our life, and through the application of daily discipline, we can choose to change anything! With the practice of gratitude, we begin to live instant to instant, always thankful, fully in the now, which is a way of totally destroying habit, as habit is a tool of the past, holding us to a pattern, and is never current. Gratitude is. Will is. Prayer is.

We change at will. We become at will. We practice gratitude at will. We decide. This means we have the power to change! Fear is a signal that we are on the right track. It shows the way. Move towards your biggest fears and move through them ... there is the biggest growth. I'm not talking about taking huge risks, putting our bodies in danger or putting our minds in the control of another. I'm talking about going *inside* and tackling the biggest resistance, looking at and naming the biggest fears, bringing them out where we can see them, and moving beyond them. Choose and grow!

It is not easy. If it were, many people would be growing and moving at a spectacular pace, yet very few are. Facing fear is the most difficult part of growth, and the most rewarding. Stick to it. Do your daily disciplines. Choose to be bigger than your fear.

It may require someone who can help you gain perspective and look at your fears without tinted glasses warping the view. I spent several years in therapy and more with a mentor developing my ability to see myself clearly and to gain detachment. I've discovered that practicing gratitude works much more quickly than therapy in giving detachment and forcing me into the now, but without the help of therapy I'm not sure I would have reached that point.

Look around for a model. Someone who seems to have what you want and who is further ahead on the path you've chosen. Ask them how they got where they are. If it makes sense, try it yourself. That is how to get beyond your present limitations and move ahead.

The most direct way to deal with the fears surrounding control is to practice gratitude. It is difficult to be concerned with control if we are totally in the now, and practicing gratitude puts us in the present moment and keeps us there. We gain detachment and awareness which allows us to see the fear and move past it. Practice gratitude daily, moment to moment, and fear will subside.

The next big fear that a lot of us have is fear of exposure, that someone will find out what we're *really* like. We fear that if they turn over the rock and see all the squiggly things, they won't like us. We fear that if we take a close look at ourselves, we won't like what we see. We fear being vulnerable and hurt because of who we are.

We learn early in life to hide our true selves so we can't be hurt. We are told repeatedly what we can and can't do and be, whether it fits us or not. "Big boys don't cry." "Girls aren't firemen." "You're a boy, don't play with dolls." "It's time you learned to get around in the kitchen, so when you grow up and get married you can take care of your husband."

Rarely, if ever, were we told "yes" when we exposed our true selves, so we hide our feelings and learn to conform. We suppress and repress anger, fear, and frustration, in order to comply with our parents. We learn quickly not to express ourselves too blatantly with our friends, as they may hold different opinions and views. We want to fit in desperately.

As we grow older, it becomes easier and easier to pretend. We conform to books' and movies' idea of reality and rarely question the validity of the "common" view. Very few people have the courage to stand up on their own. We admire them, but don't have the fortitude to go it alone. We are educated into compliance. We go to work where we fit in—our clothes fit, our hair style fits, our thoughts fit, our TV viewing habits fit, etc. We have become creatures of our society, blending in.

Yet underneath it all is an individual, with feelings, opinions, and ideas. We've been reluctant to share our personal feelings, as it exposes us to being hurt and ridiculed, especially if our feelings are not understood or accepted. We are reluctant to stand apart from the crowd, as it means responsibility for our own opinions and ideas, and usually they are not accepted by the crowd. It is easier to conform, but we know we are different, unique, and special. Maybe we've shared that with a very close friend or our spouse, but very few have seen the "real" us, because we can't take the chance it will get around. Fearing the consequences of being exposed, we perfect our camouflage and continue to conform. We keep jobs we hate, because we "should." We have a wife and child to support, or a pension to protect, or seniority to protect. What would happen if we discovered our true purpose, and wanted to go for it?

We stay in horrible relationships because of "what people would think." We pick our friends to fit in socially because "that's what other people do." Oh, we rebel on occasion, a little. We might dress differently, or hold an outlandish opinion on one issue. We build a scenario of being the leader of a new movement, or have a secret fantasy life as a hero or heroine, but it is window dressing, because we continue to keep the same base, the same self-view, and the same view of the world. Then we look at ourselves and wonder why we compromised. Why did we settle for less than we could be? Why did we go for so much less than was possible? Why can't we express the anger and frustration of feeling this way?

Fear of exposure is tied to our major fears of separation and not deserving, as is the fear of not getting what we want and losing what we have. We grasp at things to hold them tight, while we miss better things going by. Our fear contracts us, wrapped around our pain and suffering, and keeps us from opening to possibility.

We've been conditioned by our parents, education, the media, churches, and society as to what we "should" be, and we fear the judgment and criticism of others if we are different. We've been wounded before when we exposed our true feelings, so we are extremely careful and protective of ever doing it again.

It is a very difficult fear to move past, as it is subtle and takes many forms. Procrastination is probably the most insidious and damaging form of that fear we have. It is an art form with most of us. We have learned how to do it so well, we can give it other names.

We become so "busy" that we don't have time to do the important things, to take the risks in growing. We choose among the options available, telling ourselves we are taking action, but picking the easier path, the one that offers no new growth or challenge. I look back at my life and lament the chances I let go by while I procrastinated, all the opportunities lost because I had fear, the regrets that will stay with me the rest of my life from procrastination.

I look forward, and say to myself, "I want to celebrate, not explain, five years from now." I will to comfortably move past procrastination. I *deserve* to be beyond procrastinating and to receive the full bounty the universe has to offer, with no more regrets, no more hesitations and no holding back, waiting to weigh the options and make a "rational" decision. I decide there will be no more half-hearted efforts, going through the motions, being trapped in perfectionism.

Perfectionism is the ultimate trap of the procrastinator. Because we want everything to be perfect, we spend extra time and effort polishing essentially finished tasks while new opportunity passes us by. Perhaps, because we see we can't do it perfectly, we hesitate in trying at all. We lose so much from trying to be perfect, and we judge and criticize in order to rationalize our lack of effort and decision.

We say to ourselves and others that it was not "right" for us, implying that it was beneath our effort, or that it was a dumb idea. "Of course she did all right in that project, her dad owns the company." "It is really important to stick to the career path I've chosen, as all my education and experience is in that field. I'd be starting over if I tried that." "Convenience stores on every other corner to cater to people wanting to get in and out fast? Naw, it will never work." "Restaurants where people drive by a window and pick up prepared fast food? Naw, it will never work." "Studying and working at night to become more and to grow? Naw, I'll never change."

"As soon as the kids are out of school, I'll go back to work." "As soon as I'm out of debt, I'll start an investment and savings plan." "As soon as my divorce is final, I'll start looking for a new job." "As soon as my husband gets his promotion, we'll get started on the community project." *As soon as* ... where have we seen that before?

We negate and judge that which we are too afraid to risk, or we put it off. We justify our lack of action in the name of intelligence and reason. We miss so much because of our fear. We procrastinate away our chances of succeeding in what we do decide to try. In sales, we may wait all morning to get our courage up to make calls. We may wait until we are "fully prepared" in order to make a presentation to the boss on a new idea. In the meantime, someone casually mentions the idea and is given the project of developing it. We hesitate and hold back because we fear rejection, lack of control, that we don't deserve to succeed, that we'll expose ourselves as incompetent or unworthy or worse. Oh, the damage we do to ourselves in the name of fear.

In relationships, we fear so many things that we become a characters in a play, rather than a real person communicating with another. We fear getting hurt, so we hold back our real feelings and only give a little, in case we don't get any back. We've been hurt before, in past relationships or this one, so we contract around that hurt and suffering, and become rigid and stiff. We can give anger, but little else. We fear intimacy, as it means being vulnerable and open, so we manufacture little arguments and upsets so we can maintain distance between our partner and ourselves, without consciously being aware of it. Over time, we have so ritualized our relationships that there is little left of the original love and energy, and we drift apart, or it comes apart in a big explosion of pent-up emotion and hurt. Our fear keeps us from relating.

We need to move through and past our fear. We need to become familiar with the feelings of fear and know them for what they are—resistance to growth and change, signals that we are moving in the right direction. We can use our insight and awareness to see fear as a beacon guiding us on the endless path of becoming and growing.

As we grow and expand in gratitude, we begin to see that every problem and challenge has a gift in it. In fact, it is in the problems and challenges that our growth and expansion reside. We can look back at the challenges we've faced, and realize the lessons and gifts we received by moving through them. Not the problems we've avoided or pushed under, but the challenges we've met and overcome or worked through. Every one of them contained gifts and lessons. Problems and challenges are not to be feared; they are to be welcomed as opportunities to grow.

As I mentioned, it was through the challenges facing me in my second marriage that I got involved in therapy, and through therapy, in accelerated forms of spiritual growth. Without the problems in that relationship, I never would have been forced to grow and move and become more. I was pushed into new awareness by the challenge, because I moved past the fear, got help, and did some work.

Before we move on to some solutions to moving through and with fear, let's talk about fear of failure or success. We spoke a little about this fear as being tied to the base fear of separation, which it is. A lot of us get to this fear, however, through being caught up in results. Always worrying about results keeps us from living one day at a time. We identify so much with the results that we become them. We can become a workaholic, obsessed by results. We judge ourselves and others based on what they have (results) and how they look (results) and where they live (results) and what they drive (results) and how others see them (results). We lose sight of inner values and look to the outside for all validation. We fear we don't measure up, so we drive ourselves to get more and more. When we are not satisfied and made happy by getting more, we figure we don't have enough.

We know in our secret heart that we don't deserve success and we are afraid someone will expose us for the imposters we are, so we get more and work harder to get still

more. We lose sight of who we are, or, knowing that we truly
don't deserve success, we sabotage every opportunity to
move ahead. We got "held up" and were late for that crucial
meeting. We "forgot" to get the suit cleaned and pressed for
the big boss coming in from out of town. We waited until the
last minute to do that big report and did a sloppy and half-
hearted job. We just keep getting stuck on the phone and
caught up in paperwork, and can't get out of the office to
make those sales calls. Then we can't figure out why we
don't succeed.

We miss seeing the fear and the opportunity presented
by it to become more, be more, give more. We identify so
strongly with the results of what we are doing that we lose
balance in our lives. We need to come to a new awareness
in our lives about results. We spoke a little about this when
we discussed will, but it is worth repeating. We don't have
any control over results!

We can plan, research, analyze, and scrutinize results and
it doesn't change a thing—they are either there or they are
not. The only thing we have total control over is *our effort*
in achieving those results. People operate under free will.
They will choose for themselves. So, if the results involve
other people (they almost always do), then the results are out
of our hands. We can give full effort in going for results, and
have control of our effort, but the results will take care of
themselves. Release them. Do your best and let it go. Being
tied to results means we are putting our lives into the hands
of others and leaving it up to circumstance and chance to
determine who we are. Know that the reward is in the effort,
and the results will take care of themselves. Bring full
awareness to the effort, and let go.

Is it easy to do? No, but with work and practice and
becoming balanced in the now through gratitude, it is
possible. Releasing the fear of failure or success means
moving past results and seeing the value in ourselves as
unlimited children of God, deserving of all the bounty of the

universe. It is in the giving of full effort that meaning is attained. It is in giving fully in the moment that realization is attained. It is in loving completely and surrendering to the flow that God-awareness is attained.

Before we discuss surrender and love and moving completely into the flow of creation and realization, we need to discuss one more fear. That is the fear of death. Can you hear the thunder and organ music in the background? We are so melodramatic about death in the West, and we have such deeply held fears and apprehensions. We fear the unknown. We fear the end. We fear pain and suffering. We have lost touch with our humanity and our connection with the flow. We see death as an ending rather than a beginning, a transition. Even the religious views of death have us fearing judgment and retribution. We find scant comfort in moving toward death.

I was twenty years old when I stepped off the plane in Viet Nam. Physically, I was as strong and powerful as I had ever been in my life. I was a trained killer, with fast and powerful reflexes. The army had ground me down to a cog in the machine, and I was off to defend democracy. I was scared to death!

The plane ride from Oakland to Viet Nam took about twenty hours. Those twenty hours of facing the fear of death, of the unknown, fears that I wouldn't measure up, were the worst twenty hours of my life to that point.

Once I was with my unit and out in the field, it wasn't much better. Surrounded by jungle, with an enemy we couldn't see, not knowing when and if we would have to fight and possibly kill—the tension and not knowing was incredible. As I settled into the routine and rhythm of the unit and the jungle, boredom became the main enemy, with terror punctuating the fabric of the day.

Would today be the day that I die or get maimed? I shot and was shot at without seeing anything but muzzle flashes.

Mortar shells fell into our camp at night, with the roar of the gunships tearing apart the jungle in the background, bringing adrenaline flow and surge of terror. Is this it? I lied to get out of the infantry. I knew I was going to die. So, I told the army that I was an experienced photographer and writer. I thought I would be assigned to a base camp unit preparing releases for the press.

I was assigned to a base camp PIO unit, but I became a photojournalist sent to wherever the action was hottest. I jumped from the frying pan into the fire! My first assignment, however, was to write releases for the press describing the action of soldiers awarded posthumous medals. Day after day, I described the bravery of men who died in action. It was terrible and at the same time secretly rewarding work. I was still alive!

I became a decent photographer, saw a lot of action, and had many pictures published. I got to know many of the helicopter pilots who flew me in and out of the action. They were a very crazy and fatalistic bunch of people. We took crazy risks for fun, but against the background of the war, they seemed sane—flying down the river with the skids skimming the water, trying to scare the sampans into dumping, or letting me handle the 'copter, without any training, just to see if I could pick it up. It was typical of how we handled our fear.

The other way I handled the fear and boredom was to drink and dope. I didn't take the chance while in the field, but at base camp or in the rear, I drank every night and smoked weed with it. It was all very accessible and cheap. A quart of gin was only $.90 in the PX, and I had a ration card for a case of beer a day.

On my twenty-first birthday, I lay on top of a bunker with a friend at night, watching the incoming and outgoing firefight while shooting tracers into the air with a borrowed M16. I thought, if there is a God, He is crazy and beyond my comprehension to let something like this happen.

My whole tour in Viet Nam was a combination of overriding fear, boredom, and questioning. How could this happen? When am I going to buy it? Then, a fatalistic acceptance that sooner or later, it was going to happen, so I might as well party now. I looked for more risk to keep it interesting until it happened. I came home to a wife who had no idea who I was. Neither did I.

After the luxury of years to reflect, I can look back and see the gifts and lessons that I received from Viet Nam. I learned that I can survive. In the down and dirty basic survival struggle, I can get out the other side. I learned that guns don't mean strength. I was able to get rid of my guns and knives and move past thinking guns were for defense. Guns are for killing, period, and I am not a killer. I learned that I have courage. In spite of my fear, I was able to move forward and keep going.

I was given an inner awareness of my own death. I wasn't able to face it for a long time. When all the publicity surfaced about post-trauma stress syndrome, I examined myself to see why I didn't seem to have that reaction. I had gone through the alcoholic and drug days, lost two marriages, and screwed up a lot of jobs, but somehow I didn't count that as post-trauma stress syndrome. I think I would have done that without the war. What I did receive from the war was a sure knowledge of my mortality. I didn't need to wait for my mid-life crisis to face my death and learn the value of life. I know what it means to fear and survive. I know what it means to feel guilty for being alive when others around me are dying. I know the intense feeling of gratitude for being alive and being able to give some back!

From the moment we are born, we are moving toward death. Death is the natural conclusion to life in this form. We know that we are not just form, however. There is a part of us that is not made of atoms and molecules and matter, a part connected directly to the source of all life—God. We know, in our quiet moments, that there is an inner observer that watches, but is a separate Higher Self. Some of us have directly experienced the Higher Self through meditation or realization. Gratitude or another spiritual path has given some of us awareness of that greater flow that is larger than our experience in these bodies, larger than our thoughts, knowledge, or beliefs.

Death is the doorway to experiencing that flow at a different level. It is a transition to another knowing and being, and it is as natural as breathing.

Even if death is the end, looked at rationally it would still mean the same thing. It is going to end, either in form or absolutely. So what have we to gain by giving in to fear? Haven't we been deluded into thinking we're protecting something through fear, rather than being denied something? Fear limits our experience. It keeps us from being all we can be. It tells us to slow down and be safe, to conform and fit in. Fear whispers of exposure and embarrassment, and shouts of pain and suffering. Fear is a liar and a cheat! It cheats us of living fully and completely. We should get angry at fear—it is a thief! It steals our ability to experience at the peak of our powers. It is a sham and a con artist. We must move through it and past it. We must!

I have an exercise that I would like you to try concerning fear. It requires an open mind and an ability to look at fear closely. The benefits of the exercise are well worth the effort. This is how it works. First, write down your three worst fears. That's right, the ones you are most afraid of, the biggies. Now, for each fear, remember back to the last time you felt that fear intensely. Remember experiencing that fear and how it made you feel: the inner trembling, shakes, anxiety, whatever. Remember those feelings. Now, in looking back at that experience of fear, name the gift or lesson in it. Do that for all three fears. Can you see the value in this? Fear does have value, and it does contain gifts, if we are willing to look and to learn.

Let's lay to rest one more thing before we move on to love and surrender, the two sure destroyers of fear. Let's talk about pain and suffering. I'm not sure I totally understand the purposes of pain and suffering. I am moved by the suffering of children. I am outraged at the infliction of pain on man by man. I commiserate with the suffering and pain of those fighting disease and injury. I am overwhelmed with compassion for those suffering from the terror of their own minds. Yet I know there is a purpose behind it all. Whether it is the wheel of karma coming to completion or the cleansing of the soul, I can't say. I do sense that pain and suffering are methods of purifying the soul.

Some of the most peaceful and centered people I've met have been in the last painful grip of a terminal disease. Something about the pain and suffering has brought them clarity and wholeness. I feel that the pain and suffering we go through that is not connected to the death experience is also a learning process, which teaches us that we are not our bodies. We *have* a body, and that body can be very painful, but it is not *us*. The pain we experience can teach us to live in the now and release the contraction we tend to hold when in pain. It teaches us that there is more than just this, that experience in this body is limited and that we are more than that experience. Pain points the way to our death and the meaning in letting this body, this identity, this name, go. It is not us.

Whatever we believe in terms of a religion or creed, these ideas will only enhance and amplify our commitment. The practice and mastery of these principles results in becoming more powerful, purposeful, and direct. Seeing fear for what it is, and being able to move past it and through it, gives us the ability to become established in gratitude and the flow of creation.

I was in the middle of clearing and cleansing family issues, letting go of feelings and fears that weren't mine. I used letters to my parents to clean up some of these issues.

Even though my dad is dead, I wrote to him about my fear, anger, and shame, and read it out loud to him. I did the same to my mother, except I mailed it to her.

In reflecting on it, if I were to do it again, I would use a gentler method, but I was in pain and needed to let it go. My sister got a call from my mom, who read her the letter and cried about what an ungrateful and unforgiving son I was.

My sister wrote to me, very upset and angry, and asked how could I be so mean and thoughtless to my mother, for someone who professed such high principles of unconditional love and forgiveness? She told me to go to hell, and basically drummed me out of the family.

I was hurt. I wanted to write back and show my sister how I was "right" in my viewpoint and she should see it, too. Then it struck me—it is not a matter of being right. Both my sister and mother are very afraid.

Fear of change and fear of seeing and accepting a different viewpoint was keeping my mom and sister locked in an emotional knot that did not allow them to change. If they acknowledge that they have a choice, that they are not victims, then they are accountable for how they feel *now!* That is difficult for most of us. They wouldn't be able to justify the pain and fear in their lives now, and they would have to change. I jumped into an unhealthy family system that, out of fear, would rather deny the truth and remain in pain than change.

There are many more permutations of fear. We can all come up with many more examples in our lives. Fear is one of the most universal experiences. How it manifests itself is not the important issue. Becoming aware of how we avoid it, repress it, and slide around it, is the issue.

We must learn to name our fear, to be more and more aware of it, minute to minute. We must learn to become grateful for our fear and the signal it provides that here is an area for growth and expansion, a lesson, a motherlode of potential. Let go of the fear and release into the growth.

Let's go on now to some methods of moving beyond fear and resistance. These are insights and methods given to me through years of practice and through insights made instantaneous in the awakening of awareness. If you are like me, you will question these approaches. Please do!

Again, I want to remind those of you in recovery to put these methods in the context of working with the Twelve Steps. Without a solid foundation of sobriety through the Steps, it will be difficult to gain the benefits of what is offered here.

Anger

Anger is a short madness.

—Horace

Anger is so universal that we hardly ever look and examine its meaning. We all get angry, and most of us feel guilt for getting angry. Anger generates a lot of energy. We can learn to use that energy for spiritual growth.

Anger is a product of fear. We get cut off on the freeway by a rude driver. We fear there is not enough road, or that we will be late (fear we don't have enough time), or that we will lose something because of that so-and-so's action, or that our status is threatened. So we get angry. The other driver is not aware of our anger. They go about their day without it hindering them, but we simmer all day. Anger colors everything we do.

We are told "no" by mom when we are a kid. It hurts. We think she doesn't love us enough to say yes. We think we may not get what we want. We fear we don't deserve it. We fear lack of love, lack of possession, lack of time, or lack of ability to do. We get angry. We are not allowed to express our anger at mom, so we repress or suppress it. We bury it, and feel a little guilty that we got mad at mom. Years later we are having a discussion with our wife or husband and s/he says "no." Out of all proportion to the discussion, we get angry! The anger from mom's "no" gets unloaded on top of the "no" from our husband or wife. We probably aren't aware of it.

A guy at school calls me a name. I fear not being accepted. I'm insecure about my standing with my peers. I fear lack of support, separation, exposure. I get angry and aggressive. I start a fight. Or I fear getting beat up, hurt, and humiliated, so I stuff my anger and ignore the name. Maybe I make light of it with a joke and become a clown to mask my insecurity. Does any of this sound familiar? Fear and anger have many masks. It is not always easy to see them for what they are and be able to deal with them.

What causes anger? It is the resistance to fear that we manufacture. It shows itself as frustration, irritation, impatience, guilt, and many other forms, but it is anger. We feel anger because we do not accept our fear and the message that fear is giving us. Now, if our fear is based on perceived physical danger—the "fight or flight" reaction—and we are not facing actual danger, that fear has to go somewhere. Stress reaction causes great harm to the body. So does the anger generated by the kind of fear not related to physical danger—fear of separation, death (in principle), exposure, failure and success, and all its other guises. Those fears generate just as much energy as the fight or flight syndrome. We can learn to channel that energy into constructive pathways, too.

Anger is a legitimate feeling. It is a wonderful source of energy. It mobilizes us to fight injustice and unfairness. It generates the motivation to change. Only when we don't express anger in a healthy manner, or repress, suppress, or deny it, do we cause ourselves problems.

Anger is just the signal that a fear is not being accepted and recognized. When you get angry what happens to your body? Do you clench your jaw? Do you tighten your shoulders? Does your stomach hurt or get upset? Do you get a headache? If you don't express your anger, do you get depressed? Do you have ulcers or upset stomach a lot? Do you have tight and sore muscles? Do you have regular headaches? Where in your body do you carry anger?

I have different places in my body where I can feel anger with different people or situations. Anger at my mom or family is carried in my chest. Anger at my dad is carried in my gut. Anger at work is carried high in my back. You carry anger in specific places also. Learn to be aware of where you place your anger.

I had been in therapy for about a year with Ed, when he suggested I try working with his daughter Stacy in movement therapy. I was open to the idea, so I made an appointment. I had no idea what movement therapy was, but it appealed to my sense of balance to think I could use my body to heal my mind.

Stacy and I met in her studio and discussed what we would be doing. She explained that she worked with people to free their bodies of the blocks and restrictions that inhibited full use of the body. She said people tended to "hold" experience in the body until the holding became habitual. She explained how people limit their own movement and grace with this habitual holding of experience.

She asked me to stand and walk around naturally while she continued to talk with me. Then she had me stand still while she mimicked my posture. She exaggerated it so I could see the holding. She had me mirror her, and really exaggerate the position I held naturally. Then she had me release it, abruptly.

I couldn't believe it! I started to cry uncontrollably and to sob convulsively. It took me fifteen minutes to regain control. I had been holding so much anger and sorrow in my natural posture that when it was released, the emotional release was overwhelming.

What are you holding? Learn to spot the pattern of where you put your anger. Use that awareness as a signal that energy is available to put to good use. Rather than holding the anger, we will use it to move past the fear that caused it.

Take a minute now to think back to the last time you were really angry with someone close to you—your spouse or parent. Where do you feel that anger in your body? Specifically? Now, examine that part of your body with your mind. Do you habitually put anger there?

There is energy—a charge—to anger. Take that charge you just generated and replace it with the will to accept and name the fear behind the anger. What was it? Fear of rejection? Fear of loss of love? Fear of exposure? Find it and name it, then will to find the gift or lesson in it.

I go to a men's stag Twelve Step meeting very regularly. It is a good group of men with some long-term sobriety.

I had about three months of sobriety when I went to that meeting for the first time. The topic was the Third Step: "Made a decision to turn our will and our lives over to the care of God *as we understood Him.*" It was my turn to talk, and I started to explain some of my confusion with the spiritual aspects of the program. I went to treatment at an Indian center, since I couldn't afford a private treatment center and I didn't have insurance. (American Indian is a small part of my heritage.) In the Indian center, we used the medicine circle and drumming and chanting to get in contact with the spirit.

I was explaining this to the group and confessing doubt and confusion as to making a total decision to turn my will over, when a guy sitting across from me interrupted and said, "Todd, you don't have to worry about it! Indians can't stay sober anyway." The whole group laughed like crazy. On the inside I was burning up with anger. I was new to sobriety; I was new to that group; and being unsure of myself, I didn't express my anger. I was afraid he was right. I finished talking and stewed.

I told myself I would show that guy! I would stay sober and become a model of health. I would ram it down his throat in a few years! I used my anger to harden my resolve to get and stay sober.

By the way, the person who made that comment became a good friend of mine, and apologized for his remark, but it had done its work. It provided energy for me to remain sober.

It is that simple. Will to use the energy created by anger to find the source fear and reveal the gift or lesson in it. It is not easy, but it *is* simple! Just take that energy generated and released from the anger and give it to the will. Will to use it to find the gift in the fear. Will to use it in pursuing purpose. Choose to rechannel that energy, not to block it or hold it. Rechannel it into constructive powerful areas.

Try this. Sit quietly and think back to that incident where you got angry. Really feel the anger! Now, feel the spot in your body where you usually store that kind of anger. Tell that spot that this time you want to release it. Say, "Back, this time I want to release this energy. Please don't hold it." If you choose, you can release whatever held energy you possess.

Now, will that energy into your purpose or your will or into naming the gift in the fear underneath the anger.

"I *will* to comfortably unearth the fear behind this anger and find the gift in it." "I *will* to comfortably use this energy given to me by my anger to pursue my purpose." This adds tremendous power and directness to your intent. Practice this for a while until you can use it easily. It can be done.

There are two other faces of anger that I would like to address. The first one is righteous indignation. Those of us raised in dysfunctional families will recognize the importance of being right. Being right justifies all kinds of unrewarding behavior. When the ability to feel emotions has been numbed through shame and family "rules" being applied that indicate that we are "bad" because we are being treated badly, then being "right" becomes an island of security.

It is very important in my family to be right. When we are right, it is okay to get angry when someone does not recognize our "rightness." Obviously, if they were "right"-thinking people, they would see our point of view. Since they don't, they must be "wrong." In the name of being "right," it becomes possible to badger, shame, intimidate, and hurt those we love. The anger tied up in being right is misplaced from not being able to express anger in appropriate situations.

Here are some of the messages I received as a child: "Might makes right." "Parents are always right." "Parents always win the argument." "If you don't agree with the parent, you must be wrong." "Just because it doesn't seem fair, doesn't mean it isn't right." "It is right because I said so."

So, right became very important to me, as it did for a lot of you. Being right meant much more than just moral superiority. It meant control. It seems okay to have anger established in being "right" because of those messages received when we were kids.

It took me a long time to realize that "right" is a relative thing; that my being right does not mean you aren't right, too. There are many ways of seeing things, all of which can be right. Being right became just another attitude that colors how I view things, not a position of superiority. I had to choose, "Do I want to be right, or do I want to be happy?" Being right meant choosing to make others wrong, which alienates and separates. I was right most often with those I loved, forcefully, angrily right. How about you? What does being "right" cost you?

Another anger issue tied to this is eating disorders. Some experts estimate that 60% to 75% of eating disorders in this country are directly attributable to anger. Up to 75%! What does that say about our families and anger management?

I had a client, "Mary" (not her real name), who had eating problems from the time she was a child. In discussing her eating habits and when she felt compelled to binge, we discovered an interesting pattern.

Mary was verbally and emotionally abused from early in life by a dominating and controlling father. She was not allowed to show anger with her parents. By the time she was fourteen, Mary had become grossly overweight, sloppy, and destructive. I asked Mary to go back to when she could first remember eating out of control and ask why she decided to do that. She said that it was because she was angry at her father and needed to show it.

The pattern was more complex than that, of course, but the rudiments of it were plain. Mary was emotionally and verbally abused. She couldn't discern that her father was mistreating her, because she needed to maintain the "fantasy bonding" and the family rules that parents are always right, so if she was being treated badly, she must be "bad." She must deserve the treatment she received. If she was angry about the unfairness of her treatment (which she was), she couldn't express it to the person to whom she needed to express it. Again, the family rules were that you can't express anger at parents. So she repressed it.

The pattern was set. "I must be bad because I am treated badly. I am angry, but I must be wrong because parents are always right. I am angry, but I can't express anger at my parents." Mary expressed her opinion of herself by bingeing into a grossly overweight, sloppy person, just the sort of person who looked like she deserved the kind of treatment she received.

Later in life, Mary's response to anger was the same. She ate. Once she saw the pattern, and did some work with her underlying sense of self-worth, Mary was able to gain control of her eating habits and learned to express her anger in healthy ways.

It wasn't quite that simple, as Mary had other problems, but the work on her eating habits progressed very quickly once she made the connection to her anger. Take a look at your eating or not eating. Is it connected to your anger? How do you feel about food? What do you use food for?

I urge you to examine your anger patterns and how you express or don't express anger. Learn to relax into your anger, use the energy, and move past the underlying fear. Use your will and your purpose to help in channeling the energy into creative uses. Ask your Higher Self for the methods or symbols that can help you gain a different perspective on anger. It will liberate your life!

Purpose

*To have a great purpose to work for, a purpose
larger than ourselves, is one of the secrets of
making life significant; for then the meaning
and worth of the individual overflow his
personal borders, and survive his death.*
                                    —Will Durant

We already talked about action once but let's look at it
again. We said the biggest barrier to action was fear. Now
we'll say that one of the best methods of overcoming fear is
action. Of course, we will discuss other ways to approach
moving through fear and procrastination, but action is the
most direct and powerful.

Meaningful action is a result of discipline and purpose.
Discipline gains its motivation from purpose. What, then, is
purpose?

Man has always searched for meaning and purpose in life.
It is the big mystery. Why are we here? What is the meaning
of our lives? How are we supposed to find it? I will suggest
a very fine book about this search, *Man's Search for Meaning*, by Victor Frankl. Dr. Frankl was a prisoner in the Nazi
concentration camps, and discovered an interesting phe-
nomenon. Freud said that man, if reduced to his base

survival levels, would become totally instinctual, reacting as an animal. Those are the conditions the prisoners suffered in the camps. Frankl discovered that man can rise above conditions, if there is a sense of purpose.

A noble purpose, with the will established behind it, is unstoppable. It cannot be defeated; it is an irresistible force. Mahatma Gandhi had a noble purpose and an incredible will behind it. That purpose overcame the religious and geographical differences of 400,000,000 people to unite them and overthrow the British rule in India nonviolently. Martin Luther King, Jr. had the same sense of purpose and will. Jesus had such noble purpose and will that his teachings continue to inspire men after almost two thousand years.

> *I have not the shadow of a doubt that any man or woman can achieve what I have if he or she would make the same effort and cultivate the same hope and faith.*
>
> *—Mahatma Gandhi*

There are many other examples of powerful purpose and will overcoming fear, failure, defeat, hardship, and oppression. A powerful, noble purpose can drive a person forward into a compelling future. We can have that! We can develop such a drive and compelling future that we are pulled right through fear, hesitation, and hardship. We can develop a purpose.

Joseph Campbell, in his fine PBS series on myth with Bill Moyers, discussed man following his "bliss," this being the ultimate expression of man's reason for existing. Following our bliss! Discovering the heart and how we can enlarge that experience with how we live. Putting aside security and judgement and comfort, and determining that which fulfills us, then doing it!

I spent a long time searching for meaning in my life. I was confused and misdirected a lot. As I was growing up, the pain and distortion of being in a dysfunctional situation gave me no clue as to what my purpose was, other than survival.

Yet, at some level, underneath all the turmoil, I knew there was more to life than what I was seeing. As I grew into my teens, I became a voracious reader. I devoured books. I used them to escape, but I also became aware of other, larger, issues in life than my narrow concepts. School and church did not provide much comfort or direction for a person like me. I was smart enough not to be absorbed by the system and too rebellious to conform. I hurt too much and felt too ashamed to talk to anyone about the real issues in my life. By that time, I had pushed the unpleasant experiences of my abuse way back in my mind, so they were not even acknowledged. My mother was remarried, to a raging alcoholic.

I was without clear models of what being a man meant. I didn't have a clue as to what a relationship meant, except to survive and pretend. Being sensitive and hurt, I didn't know how or where to talk to anyone about it. I was a good athlete, but managed to sabotage any success I had. So I hid my discomfort, drank and drugged to get by and to fit in, and I kept reading and escaping.

Somewhere in that combination of reading, going to school, and church, I became aware of higher issues. I read Hermann Hesse's novels and resonated with the undercurrents of hidden purpose. I thought I was *Damien*. I read about the life of Mahatma Gandhi and Buddha. I prayed (not consciously, and not in a religious sense) to become a hero, or a total rebel, or both.

I got out of high school and became totally disillusioned with junior college. Of course, I didn't have the skills or the discipline driven by even a small purpose to maintain the study habits necessary to survive there, and besides, it was much more satisfying to drink and smoke. I joined the army to get out of debt and ended up in Viet Nam. I married my high school sweetheart.

What a situation for a 19-year-old with no idea what the real world was like! I learned a lot about fear and boredom in Viet Nam, and I learned a lot about liquor and dope, but I survived. Again, survival was my only purpose.

I came home to eight years of hell. I drank and doped and worked. I didn't know or care too much about anything except money to keep living my lifestyle, and power to keep from being manipulated by others. I had no idea how to nurture and honor my marriage. I was in and out of school while I worked. I eventually attended 10 different colleges before I was able to pull it together enough to get my bachelor's degree. I thought it might complete me and define me. It did neither. I swam in a sea of malaise and indifference, with an undertow of depression and pain. I had all this unnamed fear and anxiety, with nowhere to turn to find out what it meant.

I *knew* I was meant for more. I had no idea what it was. My marriage ended. I was a total failure in my own eyes. I was a waste and my life was a waste. I tried to end my life with an overdose of sleeping pills and booze, but I had built up too much tolerance over years of drinking and doping. I couldn't do it with booze and Seconal, and I didn't have the courage to use a gun.

The next year was a haze of too much booze and too many women. I was in too much pain to stop and take a look at what was happening to me, but still I knew at some level that I was meant for more. That hurt even more, that my life was the mess it was.

Then I was given a choice. Through grace, a crisis point in my life appeared where I could choose to stop drinking and move toward health, or I could keep going the way I was going and end up dead, or killing someone else, or in jail or a mental hospital. I chose to stop. I chose to move toward health and God. In making that choice, all the pieces started coming together.

Through a process of growth, therapy, work, action, the Steps, prayer, meditation, classes, searching, teachers, mentors, and finally becoming still enough to see, I became aware of my purpose. I chose to put my will behind my purpose and let the chips fall where they may! Part of the result of that decision is this book.

I don't think finding your purpose has to be as hard as I made it. In fact, I think that if a person is sincerely seeking their special niche in life, it can be fairly easy. I had, as you probably do, many things to overcome and many misunderstandings and concepts to move past. I hope my experiences and the suggestions in this book will help make your path smoother.

Victor Frankl proposes that a purpose needn't be big or noble in order to be compelling and effective. My challenge to you is: find a **big** purpose. Find a noble undertaking for your life. Don't cheat yourself into settling for a smaller challenge that won't force you to grow. Was Mahatma Gandhi a big man to begin with, or did the compelling nature of his purpose, combined with his will, *make* him big? I think it is a combination of both, and that the most important was the noble purpose pulling him into becoming more and larger, so he could be the instrument of completion of that purpose.

A noble purpose is enlarging. It always involves service to others, sharing and giving the fruits of our labor, expanding with and because of our purpose.

I have chosen what I hope is a noble purpose. I have chosen to teach gratitude. The insights I've gained from practicing gratitude and all its many combinations with will and forgiveness are compelling and life-changing. I need and want to share this with others. It is a higher purpose than just making a living or doing this part-time while I spend energy doing something else. I must share gratitude. I am in my element sharing gratitude, and I love it. It is compelling and fulfilling. It is my bliss.

The turning point for me came when I took action without being invested in the results. I was in business for myself and joined a group of people in the same business in a growth class (the class I mentioned when talking about a budget). The purpose of the class was to build our businesses to high-profit levels of income, but we really focused on personal growth. All the information being offered in the class was "old" to me. I found myself saying things like "I tried that a few years ago and it didn't work," or analyzing or judging why something wouldn't work before I had tried it. I got disgusted with myself and made a decision. I decided to do it! Period. All the exercises suggested and all the homework. I made a pact with myself not to question anything until after I had tried it for a month.

The growth I experienced was incredible! Every area of my life expanded and developed and my purpose gained sharp focus, all because I put auditing and analyzing life aside, and lived it.

How do we find our bliss? Where do we find the purpose that can drive us and pull us through fear and doubt?

I'm going to describe an exercise that will help put things in perspective for you. I am going to ask some questions that will require some soul-searching to answer. When you are through this process, you will have a pretty good idea of your purpose, and it will match what you already know, at some level!

Get a few blank sheets of paper and a pen so you can jot down your thoughts. You are going to explore some of the areas that are most important in your life and you will want to keep track of what is discovered.

Assume you had a doctor's appointment yesterday morning and he/she asked you to take some routine tests. Later that day, the doctor asks you back in to take another test. Your anxiety level is rising. The doctor says there was an unusual result on one of the earlier tests, and they just wanted to get a better and clearer picture if it might be something to worry about. Later that afternoon, the doctor calls you in and says that he/she is sorry, but there is no doubt, you have a rare and incurable disease that moves very quickly. You have only six months to live! There will be little or no pain, and it will only be the last week that you will be incapacitated and have to be in the hospital. You are absolutely stunned!

Now, assuming you learned of your disease yesterday, and have had a day to recover from the shock, it is time to decide what to do with your last six months. Who will you see? Who will you spend time with? What will you do? Where? Are there any important projects that need to be completed? Any lasting legacies that must be done?

Write out what you would do and be for the last six months of your life, if it were to start today.

Pretty interesting, yes? This lets you see very quickly where your priorities lie.

What do you love to do? If you didn't have to work for a living, what would you do? If you could have the perfect job, what would it be? If you could start over, what would you be?

It is not easy to take a hard and honest look at your life and to see what it amounts to, to take a look at what you are doing now and see if it matches your abilities and talent. When you did the exercises, what jumped out at you? What single thing or combination of things gave you a charge? Was it family, church, service, art, business?

I would suggest to you that one or two areas are going to have the deepest significance. From these areas will come your purpose. Perhaps it will be to raise and expand a family that embodies wholeness and health in all areas of life. Perhaps it will be to model in business the balanced person who can be successful while at the same time giving and sharing with the community and family. Maybe it will be to give and share love in as many forms as possible through the charity and auspices of your church. It will be what resonates and builds your energy.

In the program, we say "Pray for potatoes, but first pick up a hoe." This statement puts purpose in perspective.

Faith is our willingness to surrender to the flow of universal laws, to trust the process, and to open to the potential. Without faith, we will never start.

The hoe is our will. It is our intent, through discipline put into action. We will to do the work, every day. We put our intent into action in a meaningful way—hoeing the row, picking the weeds, working the ground, whatever it takes. The soil is our talent and potential, our inclinations and experience, our knowledge and energy. It is the home for the seed.

The seed is our purpose, the crop that we see in the future. It is the meaning for using the soil and picking up the hoe. We plant the seed and tend the soil, but the results are in God's hands. God provides the seasons, the weather, moisture, and sunlight, warmth and air. So the fruits of our labor are dependent on both God and us. We must put in the work and effort. God provides the rest.

If we have chosen the wrong seed, one that does not work well in our soil of talent, experience, and potential, we will have a poor crop. If we did not tend the soil with our hoe, putting the power of the will behind our purpose and performing the small disciplines daily that move toward our purpose, we will have a poor crop. If we planted in the wrong season, we will have a poor crop. However, seasons are cyclical. Summer always follows spring, fall follows summer, and so on. A time to plant always comes around again.

If we have chosen our seed well, tended the soil, and the seasons have been kind, we will have a bumper crop to harvest, to share and to reap the fruits of purpose—a message of faith and work.

Let's try one more exercise. We are going to call upon the Higher Self for inspiration and help in defining our purpose. We will do it in the form of a meditation. Have someone read this to you or tape it.

Find a comfortable spot to either sit or lie down. Slow your breathing and let it come easy and free. Let your thoughts drift—no hooks, no grasping—just easy, gentle flow. Relax. Nice and easy now. Gentle breath. Relaxed body.

Now connect with your Higher Self, that part of you with higher wisdom, full of compassion and love and grace, light and warmth. Feel yourself open to the presence of the Higher Self. Feel the flow of love and warmth, light and humor and joy. Openness and acceptance. No judgements. No expectations. No demands.

Ask your Higher Self to give you symbols, visions, and words for your purpose. Let the flow of these symbols, words, and pictures fill you up. Ask for the vision to expand. Let the flow of these gifts move through you for a few minutes.

Now, ask for the symbols and pictures and words to show what your purpose will be when you've expanded and grown and are capable of giving more. Take a few minutes to let these flow into you.

When you are ready, ask the Higher Self to give you a symbol or a few words that express the theme of your purpose and what you've experienced. Think of it as a way of giving simple expression to your purpose.

After receiving your theme, ask the Higher Self to give you a symbol or word for the biggest obstacle or block in moving into your purpose.

Relax now and take your time in moving fully back into this awareness. Feel yourself full of your purpose and its symbols. Know that you can always return to ask the Higher Self for clarification and help.

Take time now to define your purpose. In one or two sentences, broadly or with focus, define what it means to you to live. Where is the meaning in your life?

From this definition will come all the power, direction, and impact for our goals. The power of a purpose is what pulls us through and past fear. It is the driving force in moving toward God and the plenty the universe has to offer. Purpose cannot be ignored.

If you are having difficulty in getting to a sense of purpose, then relax and put your will to work. Will to have your Higher Self and God help you to define your purpose. "I, —————, a deserving child of God, will to comfortably define my purpose in life by next week." Relax. Let your Higher Self help you move into purpose. It *will* happen.

Don't make this a big intellectual and analytical exercise. Go with your intuition and feelings. Your heart will let you know when you are on the right track. Also, don't be surprised if things change. As we grow and expand, we become capable of larger purposes. Life and the universe always have bigger challenges for those who dare! Mahatma Gandhi did not begin his mission fully in India until he was thirty-seven. Jesus did not begin his ministry as Christ until he was thirty. Mohammed did not write the Koran until he was in his forties. A true noble purpose may take time maturing and coming into focus. Make sure you do the groundwork!

If you choose to, you can write out a mission statement. There is a lot of business literature right now that has information about companies defining their mission—how they do business. "IBM means service," for instance. We can do the same thing as individuals. If it is easier for you to work with it in those terms, rather than as a sense of purpose, then try defining your mission. Either way will work. It can be a fluid situation, especially if you are growing fast. Be open and flexible. Your heart and Higher Self will show you the way.

A noble purpose, imbued with sacredness and power, is the path to becoming more. Tarthang Tulku, in his book *Skillful Means*, talks about a noble purpose in work. In a Zen context, even the simplest tasks can be part of a noble purpose.

No matter what we choose to do for a living, we can charge that work with the energy of our purpose. If we are in sales and choose to make our purpose moving toward God, then we can make every sales contact a meeting with God. We can make every task one that moves us into sacredness. We can decide to make anything a step along the path we choose. *How* we perform a task defines its purpose.

A noble purpose is enlarging and expanding. In moving into the purpose, others receive benefit. A noble purpose is uplifting and inspiring. A saint's purpose to make every breath a prayer of thanksgiving is so simple, yet compelling.

It doesn't matter what we choose to do for a living, if we make every act a reflection of God's love. Only you can define what is the noble purpose in your life, then decide, through the will, to make it happen!

My purpose developed into teaching and sharing gratitude. Every act and task, I try to do with gratitude. I breathe gratitude and meditate gratitude. I give gratitude to everyone I can, and teach others to share it also. My purpose enlarged me. It expanded and compelled. It moves me in becoming more, giving more, having more, and being more. The noble purpose I've chosen is an act of will and a magnet. I chose to move toward God with gratitude and gratitude draws me toward God.

Be bold! Move past your fear and choose a noble purpose for your life. Whether you believe it is an act of your free will or an act of finding God's will for you, look for that purpose. Let it draw you into growing and expanding in order to fulfill it, with every action and task.

When we start this process of determining a noble purpose and move closer and closer to it, the universe gives us more and more help. Goethe said: "[T]he moment one commits oneself, then providence moves too. All sorts of things occur to help one that would never otherwise have occurred. Whatever you can do, or dream you can, begin it. Boldness has genius, power, and magic in it. Begin it now."

A noble purpose rallies the energies of the universe behind us, and the infinite wisdom and grace of God become more and more apparent. It requires making a decision and committing to it. Every part of our life will reflect it. It will be the underlying foundation of all to follow. It will define us. It is compelling and magnetic. We are different people because of our purpose.

Here is where true spiritual awakening occurs. When a noble purpose is put into action, expansion occurs, always, no doubts and no exceptions. It is the recipe for moving toward and into God, becoming all that we can, capable of giving love and energy, true charity and sharing. Purpose enlarges our potential and allows us to become the true reflection of God in the area we've chosen. What a gift and opportunity, and what a tremendous responsibility! We can choose. If we don't, we are short-changing our opportunity to grow toward God and to reach our potential. It is our choice, and we must take responsibility for it.

Please, look for your noble purpose. Make the choice and start living it. It will pull you into new dimensions of being and knowing.

The dictionary gives one of the definitions of "noble" as: having or showing high moral qualities or ideals: lofty. I would suggest that it means even more in the context of purpose. A noble purpose includes having a higher goal than just personal gain or profit. A noble purpose includes giving or sharing with others. It includes the potential for helping others, through material gain, spiritual enlargement, or for the increased dignity of all. A noble purpose contains a component of one of those elements.

I think it also includes the expression of unconditional love. Somehow, a noble purpose spreads love. Through the unselfish action of another, working through the expanding net of purpose, love is given as a reflection of God's love. In compassion, acceptance, grace, openness, and the many other forms of God's love, we manifest our purpose.

Mother Teresa of Calcutta is a very good example of a noble purpose expanding and fulfilling a person and making her a reflection of God's love. What a wonderful and sharing thing she is doing for the poor and leprous of India! Now she is sharing with many other areas of the world, through her Order. She chose to surrender completely to her purpose, and became a perfect instrument of God's love in that area.

It is not just the noble purpose that is important. It is giving to it completely, in every aspect of life, that completes the purpose and expands the person. It is an act of total surrender.

I know that sounds odd when we've been discussing free will and the ability to make choices. However, power, directness, impact, and completeness are gained from the act of surrender. The love contained in the noble purpose is the expanding component. It is the reflection of God's love which draws us into the purpose and gives an inexhaustible supply of love, compassion, empathy, and all the other elements of God's love to share. We become an instrument through which God's love, healing, and compassion can flow. Our moving into a noble purpose creates the instrument. Our surrender to the purpose opens the flow.

We use our wills to determine the noble purpose. We decide the extent and nature of our commitment to it, and how far we allow the purpose into our lives. We are in control of our growth. But once we move toward a noble purpose, unless we move completely and totally, we cheat ourselves and the universe out of being and giving what we can become. In surrendering to the purpose, we perfect the instrument of expansion and sharing, and open the floodgates of God's love.

It is truly liberating and expanding—and it brings up a lot of fear. The people who do it stand out so clearly.

You are capable of a noble purpose. Search your soul and pray for help in discovering your purpose. Do the exercises and contemplate the necessity to expand and grow to your potential. Then find a noble purpose! Own it and surrender to it. Let it lead you into fulfilling your potential and greatness, God's gift to us all. Join the purpose of others, if it is similar to yours. Move with the expanding purpose and larger momentum, when it is possible. Maybe your purpose is to be a cog in a larger machine.

In finding our purpose, be it noble and big, or of smaller proportion but no less important, it is necessary to think how we will put it into action. What will we do, on a daily basis, that moves us into our purpose? Over the next six months, one year, and five years, what specific actions do we plan to implement that reflect our purpose? Here is where the will, again, helps us move into action. We can make and practice will statements that promote our purpose, as we discussed earlier. For example, I could say:

> *I, Todd Weber, a deserving child of God, will to comfortably teach gratitude and forgiveness to my work group twice a month through April.*

> *I, Todd Weber, a deserving child of God, will to comfortably build my speaking and workshop engagements nationwide by June.*

> *In return, I, Todd Weber, a deserving child of God, will to comfortably **give** service, discipline, compassion, and love in abundance to all, beyond expectation of return.*

Let's look at the elements of these will statements. First, I reminded myself and God and the universe that I am a deserving person. Next, I invoked the will in putting its power behind my statement. Then, I used the word "comfortably." Edith Stauffer taught me to do that. If we affirm or will things, especially if they are not already present in our lives, we tend to question and negate them at lots of levels. So we include "will" to put intent and power into the statement, and we use "comfortably" so that it doesn't have to be painful or questioned and negated.

There are lots of folks who buy into the axiom "No pain, no gain," or "Pain is the touchstone of spiritual growth." I don't agree. A lot of growth *is* painful, but it doesn't always have to be. Including "comfortably" in our will statements allows the universe to find paths of growth and expansion that don't always include pain.

The last part of the will statement includes specific action we will provide over the next period of time chosen. This action is in line with our purpose and can be broken down to specific daily actions that we can discipline into our routine. We don't want to leave our purpose exposed to chipping away from lack of action and loss of motivation. By willing to put into action daily activities, we renew and reward ourselves daily through discipline. We pick up the hoe!

The last will statement is the acknowledgement of the effort we are willing to give back to the Universe in return for the power of building our purpose. We can control our effort and intent. We must release the results and move on. This statement reminds us that we can *give!* It is in the giving that our service, compassion, discipline, and love are reflected.

Will statements are powerful instruments of purpose. I have received many wonderful gifts and moved rapidly ahead in following my purpose by using will statements. I was taught traditional goal-setting techniques years ago and have updated those skills as new methods have been devised, but none has been as powerful as will statements. Will statements do not take the place of planning. They are how the planning is implemented.

Try writing out your will statements that reflect the next six months to a year. Write out four or five statements that put your purpose into action. Then just like the deserve statements (see *The Next Step Workbook*), write them out every night ten times each for two weeks. Tape them on a cassette and listen every chance you get. Repeat them once a day to a trusted friend, spouse, or mentor. Put your will behind your purpose, and you will be unstoppable!

This is how fear is defeated, how we move through and past our procrastination and hesitation. By having a powerful purpose and putting our will behind it, we are pulled into action and compelled to complete our intent. The purpose is so large that it attracts us into becoming larger. We become the instrument capable of completing our purpose. One day at a time, through the use of our will and discipline, we grow and expand through the action that moves us closer to our purpose. It is inevitable, *if* we do it.

By surrendering to the purpose, the discipline and power become available day by day. It is a paradox that we move in line with God's will through the use of our will in finding and following purpose—especially a noble purpose. Here is how it works.

Through the use of our will we decide to grow and expand. We decide to find our purpose. We use will and purpose to put our intent into action daily, then we surrender the results. This is the hardest part, and the most crucial. We spoke about this a little when we were talking about fear. Most of us gain identity and status from results. In pursuing and expanding with a purpose, the results are God's. We are the instruments of God's love flowing out to others. Our will allows control of our effort and intent. We can choose to give our best effort, to put our action in line with our purpose, and to practice daily the small disciplines leading to completion and fulfillment of our purpose. The results are God's.

Our will allows choices for ourselves. Others operate from free will too. They also have choices. The greatest gift an individual receives from God is free will. The greatest gift man, as a whole, receives from God is God's will. Humanity is a combination of all the individual free will. It is a sea of desire, purpose, and need. The mass movements of humanity are influenced by the harmony of man's free will with the universal love of God's will. The closer we are to moving into and with the flow of God's love, the more likely our purpose will resonate with the flow of the universe.

When we *decide* to move with purpose, God also moves. If our purpose is noble, then God's flow of love and help is magnified and enhanced. We are supported and enlarged by the purpose. We become conduits of God's universal love to all. If we move into our purpose with no conditions, expectations, or demands, then God moves with us. We surrender to the process and move into the flow of grace and love with no fear, no hesitation, no defeat, no negativity. Even temporary setbacks are viewed for what they are: learning experiences and gifts allowing us to regroup and renew.

Dare to think big! Ask God for direction in moving into a purpose. Look to grow into the purpose. Let God's grace pull you into the love and action necessary to be more, give more, and expand more.

We have amazing potential, and it is disappointing to see how few strive for it. We have so many excuses and judgements, so many people and circumstances to blame. In the end, what does it amount to? A wasted and futile life spent hoping, not doing. We can decide to be bigger than that. We can choose a purpose.

Robert Schuller, in his philosophy of possibility thinking, talks about dreaming without limits. If you could do anything, with no limits, what would you do? If you could be anything, with no limits, what would you be? If you could give anything, with no limits, what would you give? Find the purpose behind those dreams and begin it today!

It won't be easy, but hardships sharpen us and give us focus. Setbacks and small defeats define and refine the purpose. Each step back is an opportunity to learn and gain new perspective. Each step forward reinforces and builds power and impact. Surrender to the purpose and gain the total strength of its intent. Go with the flow of God's love and feel the intensity and nurturing of the unfolding of creation. We are the instruments of God's miracles, and it takes *action* and *purpose* to make that happen.

Meditation And Prayer

Who comes from prayer a better man, his prayer is answered.
                                        —*George Meredith*

Prayer and meditation are the means of checking out our purpose and will. Through them, we can sense directly the alignment of our purpose with the flow of God's love. In *The Next Step Workbook*, I speak about prayer being used as a tool of thanksgiving and for strengthening the will. Another good source of prayer and thoughts on prayer is the *12 Step Prayer Book* (Glen Abbey Books 1990). I feel that a prayer of thanksgiving is the most powerful prayer we can offer.

I am not putting forward religious opinion or dogma. These practices of purpose, gratitude, prayer, and meditation can be used in the context of any religion or spiritual pursuit. I am offering the fruits of my spiritual search, and the experiences and awareness that have been given to me through the practice of gratitude. Prayer and meditation have been a large part of that practice.

You may already have a meditation and prayer practice. If you don't, there are many good books available, as well as excellent centers throughout the country where you can learn to meditate. I am going to limit my comments to ways in which you can modify your existing practice or start a very simple one. In my experience, the simpler we keep our practice, the more likely it is that we will keep practicing daily. In the Eleventh Step, prayer and meditation are discussed. In the Big Book, meditation simply means quiet time. What we are talking about here is a more aggressive method.

My daily practice goes like this: I get up very early, shower, shave, clean my teeth, and put on clean loose clothes for meditation. I have a special spot in my home for meditation and prayer. The energy there has built up from the practice and is very special. I light a couple of candles and prepare myself for meditation with prayer.

My prayer is of gratitude for the day and all it contains. I pray in thanksgiving for my body and all its senses, for my mind and its capabilities, and for family, friends and experience. I also pray in gratitude for any other aspect of living that strikes me that day. I then ask for help in keeping my will strong and in line with God's love and flow. I ask for help in maintaining the power of my purpose and for the ability to give and share without holding back. I pray for the removal of any hindrances or hooks that hold me back from moving toward God. I thank God once again for the day and ask for help in filling it wisely. I am then ready for meditation.

Having reminded myself where the love and power flows from, I settle into my meditation position and remember to "Be still and know that I am God." I then follow my breath in and out while I empty myself of any expectations, demands, or conditions. I let go and open to the possibility. I go with the flow of God's love and the eternal change and unfolding of creation. I am in touch with that part of me that is and knows God. I expand into the flow. If I am having trouble letting go and releasing conditions or expectations or demands, I concentrate on my breathing. I try to release all holding and grasping. I imagine having no name, no identity, no image. I remind myself that even a rusty pipe can carry clean water, and concentrate on letting God's love flow through me without hindrance.

I finish meditation with a prayer of thanksgiving—a wish for God's love to shower on all beings this day with grace and joy.

When I am through with meditation and prayer, I review my will statements and do my gratitude exercise, if I am working on that this month. If not, I review my list of blessings. If I am doing an irritation exercise this month, I do it then. I finish by reviewing my purpose and what I am doing today to make that purpose a reality. I review my vows (we'll discuss these later).

It is a powerful and loving way to start the day. It takes me about an hour or so, including the cleansing. I find I don't miss the sleep I gave up in order to have the extra time needed. Meditation provides energy, as does the practice of gratitude. My sleep patterns keep changing as I get further and further into my spiritual practice, but I find I need less and less sleep as I progress.

In the evening, before going to sleep, I review the day and thank God for all the lessons contained in it. I read something inspiring or spiritual immediately before going to sleep so that my subconscious has positive information to ponder overnight. During the day, when I can, I remember gratitude and purpose, stay in the now, and move with the flow.

If you are just starting a practice, I suggest doing a simple gratitude prayer and meditation in the morning and evening. Include a prayer for the will to help move into purpose and maintain that purpose throughout the day. This simple prayer and meditation is very powerful and will help you immediately. To make it more direct, practice the gratitude list daily for a month. It will bring you into the flow and sense of creation and the expanding gifts of the universe. It will keep you in the now.

There are no "shoulds" in following a spiritual practice. Follow your heart and the intuition you receive from your Higher Self. They will direct you in the ways of moving into the flow which are best for you. If you are having difficulty starting or maintaining a practice, seek out a mentor or teacher, someone who seems to have what you want and appears to be further down the path you wish to travel. Don't be afraid to change teachers or mentors if they move you in a direction that is uncomfortable or hurtful.

On the other hand, don't be too quick to change teachers if the teaching is leading you into confronting the resistance within yourself. That resistance can be uncomfortable, also. Trust your intuition and ask God for help if you are unsure if you are on the right path or with the right teacher. A teacher or mentor can accelerate our rate of growth tremendously and help us past the hang-ups and pitfalls we all face along the way. However, a teacher is not necessary; it is our choice. Either way, through a teacher or on our own, if we surrender to our purpose and to the flow of God's love within, with gratitude, we can move toward God and the completion of our spiritual path.

We use prayer and meditation to keep in contact with our Higher Self and to draw on that sense of purpose and strength that is given to us through the flow. We become the perfect instrument of God's love, allowing that love to flow through us to all who need it. Our purpose gives the means to express that love. It is a wonderful and fulfilling gift, and it only requires a little work daily to maintain it.

I was talking with a friend recently and she pointed out to me that whenever I spoke the "truth" there were contradictions in my expression. We discussed it for a while, and this is what I discovered. We are spiritual beings in a physical overcoat. We have this wonderful body and mind to play with and learn from. Part of the learning is that emotional and intellectual truths are different and paradoxical, as are physical truths. On a higher plane altogether are spiritual truths. We reflect the higher truths in the linear intellectual truths, but it cannot encompass all the truth because of limits of thought, belief, and knowledge.

A concept such as "purpose is a choice and a surrender," although it seems a paradox, reflects that higher truth. "Power comes from the use of our will in line with God's will" is also a paradox, when dealing with the concept of free will. It is not a matter of "understanding," but of going with the intuitive knowledge of the heart that feels truth. We are so limited in the way we can view the universe and God that it is a wonder we have useful concepts at all.

Prayer and meditation are ways to get in touch with that higher truth and knowledge. We use prayer to move toward God through gratitude and to ask for help in proper use of the will. We use meditation to open to the flow of God's love.

Limits

Every man takes the limits of his own field of vision for the limits of the world.
—Schopenhauer

From the moment we are born, we are trained and educated to become limited beings. We come from a totally open and love-full spiritual dimension. We are so open and free when we are born that there is no separation between us and our environment. In fact, it is not until around the age of 18 months, according to child psychologists, that we really establish the concepts of "me" and "out there."

We are born into a limited physical reality, limited in the sense of what we can perceive in this body, limited in the sense of time, and limited in the way we use our minds. Even with modern technology, we can only see a small portion of the spectrum of light wavelengths, hear a small portion of the sound wavelengths, and feel a small portion of the vibrational wavelengths. Our sense of the flow of energy in the universe is basically limited to the difference between hot and cold, solid, liquid, and gas.

We came from an unlimited spiritual dimension, to which we will return. When we are born, we still have a sense of that unlimited plane. Most of us lose that memory or knowledge. Some do not, and some regain it.

However, for those of us who did not maintain contact with that unlimited portion of our spiritual being, we must learn to move in our limited environment to become unlimited beings. It is quite a challenge at one level, and at another is no challenge at all, since we are already established in the flow of unlimited love and creation.

As we grow, we are given beliefs, limits, and rules. At first, we are limited physically. We are given certain areas where we can operate; others are off limits. There are certain things we can do with our hands, and others we cannot. There are certain types of behavior that are "acceptable," and others which are not. We are taught to limit bodily functions until more appropriate times. Then we start to learn the "rules." Obviously, a lot of what we learn at this time is necessary to get along in this society and to function as a balanced human being.

What we need to look at now is how each one of these experiences, beliefs, rules, and learning limited the direction and content of further learning and expansion. It is estimated that humans use less than 10% of the capacity of the brain. By some estimates, we use much less. Yet, it is also thought that the ability of the brain to store and use information may be virtually unlimited! Why do we use so little of our potential?

As we grow, and usually before the age of four, we absorbed the belief structure operating in our family. Some of these beliefs are spoken and some of them are not, but all that we learn and experience from then on is limited by that belief structure. Here are just a few typical, unquestioned beliefs that we may operate with: "life is a struggle," "there is never enough," "don't trust anybody," "don't talk back," "children are seen and not heard," "it is important to be right," "big boys don't ... ," " big girls don't ... ," "a lady acts like ... ," " a gentleman acts like ... ," "might makes right," "other races are less than," "God is on our side," "that is a sin, and God hates sinners," "only our faith is the right one," "you can't be too careful," and many, many more. Usually we don't examine those beliefs, they just keep operating in our lives and continue to limit all that we see, do, and hear, affecting all new experience and learning.

As we grow and mature, we become aware of other "truths" and some of our beliefs change. Yet, underneath it all are the unexamined core beliefs continuing to operate. As we gain experience and knowledge another factor comes into play. Since we are bombarded daily with millions of bits of information, the mind must distinguish which is most important and which isn't. Only a small percentage of the information sensed can be brought to conscious attention, so a priority system is in place. The first priority is survival, so any information that shows threat to survival is given priority. We all have read, heard, and experienced the problems created by that in this society, with the devastating results of stress.

The mind then creates other priorities, through the reticular activating system, as to what is brought to conscious awareness and what isn't. Most bodily function information is left at an unconscious level. Most sensory input information is left unconscious. Only the place where we turn our attention is brought to awareness. So, we program ourselves as to what we make conscious and what we leave unconscious. Our goals, beliefs, previous experiences, knowledge, and attitudes all influence how we filter information, and once it is brought to conscious awareness, it is judged and evaluated based on all previous experience similar to it, and by our beliefs and attitudes concerning that type of experience.

As we grow older and "wiser," the most common thing that happens is that we grow less and less in our insight as we judge more and more by prior experience. That is why every spiritual practice has a warning and a hope that we can be as little children, open and accepting, without judgement, conditions, or demands.

If we are to expand beyond our current limits, we must open up again to new beliefs and experiences. We must take a look at our current beliefs and be willing to move past them if they are limiting. Every belief is limiting!

It is hard for us to accept that we have chosen voluntarily to limit our lives, yet that is what most of us have done. If we had toxic parents or a dysfunctional family background, then we really must examine the sabotaging and self-defeating beliefs that we generated from that experience and discard them.

As I've said, I was raised in a dysfunctional family. Part of the insidious nature of some dysfunctional families is the double life that is presented. On the outside, we were a good, middle-American family. We went to church, the kids did well in school (most of us, anyway), we played sports, and all the other family things. We appeared to be typical, and we were given typical American values by our parents. Yet, there was conflict between what was said and what was done.

I was told over and over again that big boys don't cry. (I must have cried a lot!) If you are hit and get hurt, don't cry—get even. Over and over again I was told to be a "man." It is acceptable for a man to express his anger (except against his parents!), but not his pain or fear. I had some very strong beliefs as to what it meant to be a "man." It wasn't until I was in therapy in my thirties that I realized what those beliefs had cost me, and the terrible price of learning, as an adult, how to be emotionally expressive and receptive of others' expressions of emotion with compassion, openness, and acceptance.

Those beliefs were very limiting, yet I had not examined them closely until a crisis period in my life forced me to. That is when most of us look at beliefs—when the pain becomes great enough that we have to do something, anything, to make it stop!

Even if you had a wonderful upbringing, much of what we learn when we are little is distorted and out of date with our spiritual pursuit. It is worth the time and trouble to re-evaluate where we stand. We are going to be moving forward from here. So, please take a look at what you believe. Is it building value in your life, or is it limiting and damaging to your growth?

We will be changing our perceptions through the use of the will, in order to move into an unlimited understanding of our place in the universe and as children of God. Through practice, we will move past beliefs and perceptions that hold us back and sabotage our efforts. Being grateful for past experience and belief, and being able to see the lessons and gifts in them is a great place to start. If you haven't done a gratitude exercise in awhile, now is a great time to do one.

Gratitude is the quickest way to the Higher Self, and through the Higher Self we gain an unlimited view of the universe. In order to expand and grow, we use the will to maintain our contact with our Higher Self and to maintain our purpose. When we surrender to our purpose, we open to the possibilities and potentials of unlimited expression, and *allow* the method of expression and the results of the expression to be unlimited by our beliefs and thoughts. We give our Higher Self rein to move at will.

This is where we purify our will as an instrument to move with and toward God. Until now, we've been creatures of habit, comfort, and meaningful but limited intent. Now is the time to unleash the power of our purpose and remove the limits of our intent. The will is the means for moving beyond our current boundaries.

By using prayer, meditation, and will statements, we remove the limits to our purpose. Have you discovered your purpose? Have you explored the vastness of the flow of love from God and determined your expression of it? Do you know the meaning of your life?

No? Or yes? Either way, let's take a look at some methods for sharpening our skills and opening to the unlimited nature of our purpose and how we can express it. The will is the instrument of change. If you are not sure of your purpose, then will to become aware. If you are sure of your purpose, then will to put it in focus for action.

We discussed will statements in the section on the will and when we discussed purpose. We are going to look at them again, in a different light, and then expand to a new way of using the will.

Will statements are an invocation of the will. They are a method to focus the will and to move into accord with our Higher Self, which is powerful and effective. However, I must caution you again, do not be hung up on results! We are moving into an unlimited arena for growth and action. What we consider proper or necessary results may not even be in the frame of the flow the universe sends us through the use of our will. Don't judge the exercise or the universe based on your expectation of what "should" result. Be open for what *does* result.

Will statements are very similar to deserve statements, except that they invoke the will and are totally open in their expression. In other words, try not to limit the workings of the will or the universe by the wording used in the will statement. Of course, it is a big conceit to think that our words can limit the universe, but it is our **perception** of the universe that is being limited. Here are some examples of my new will statements. Look carefully at the wording.

> *I, Todd Weber, a child of God, will to comfortably be spiritually dynamic and growing.*

> *I, Todd Weber, a child of God, will to comfortably expand my practice of gratitude into unconditional surrender to the flow.*

> *I, Todd Weber, a child of God, will to comfortably develop purpose through the*

will into a powerful, unstoppable force!

I, Todd Weber, a child of God, will to comfortably be financially unlimited through the pursuit of my purpose.

I, Todd Weber, a child of God, will to comfortably reflect the unconditional love and grace of my Higher Self in all my relationships.

*In return, I, Todd Weber, a child of God, will to comfortably **give** service, discipline, compassion, and love in abundance to all, and beyond expectation of return.*

By invoking the power of the will, and stating the objectives of my growth, the whole thrust of my being is centered on becoming that spiritual instrument. I have not limited my growth by stating **how** I will grow or **how** fast. I have tried to open the boundaries. Of course, will statements change fairly often. As we grow and integrate the expansion into the actions of life, the perception of our will statements changes and we revise them or modify them. Growth is so dynamic and powerful, that those statements may change every week or once every three months. That depends on how hard we push it.

Each of the will statements is a new way of defining and limiting the flow. It is through growth and expansion that our perception of the flow changes and our will statements change. The statements are merely a method for building awareness and realization of what is already there. We are unlimited children of God. We are already established in the flow of God's love. We all are; it is just our awareness and perception that is limited. The will statements help to expand that awareness and let it manifest itself in our lives. This is where true expansion and power is generated, in the knowledge of what is already established.

Many of us have difficulty with this concept and exercise. In discussing the will and in the section on purpose, I did this exercise of will statements with time constraints and more limited use of the will. Perhaps you too will feel more comfortable doing it that way, rather than jumping into an unlimited perception immediately. I started with small bites.

I'd been working will statements for about six months, writing them out every morning with my gratitude list. I did each statement three times, just to keep it fresh in my mind as I went about the business of the day. I had statements that were pretty limited in scope, like: *I, Todd Weber, a child of God, will to comfortably be spiritually active and growing, giving three or four workshops this year. I will meditate every day until August 1.*

I had five statements that were very similar. One day, it became apparent to me that I was in a place that had no limits, a flow of God's love without dimension, with potential, energy, time, experience, knowledge all flowing in a matrix that I was observing and being at the same time. It was a place without the constraint of words, of direct and powerful expression, of openness and expansion, of grace, and of unlimited possibility.

I didn't stay in that flow all the time. I was able to get to it with gratitude and maintain it longer and longer through practice in gratitude throughout the day. It opened me and pulled me into a new way of being. Each day I am re-created in the flow and emerge a new person. Each day I become more than I was yesterday in my perception, as I expand and grow with the practice. The only limits are my own, and those, too, are part of the flow. God's gifts to us are never-ending, if we are open.

My will statements started changing to reflect unlimited use of the will, and have continued to change as my awareness changes.

This practice is a process, a continuum of increasing awareness and perception that moves us into being established in the flow always. There are no limits. We can give totally, and be blessed with the open bounty of the universe.

When we surrender to our purpose, the higher use of the will becomes apparent and moves us into that awareness of the flow. Surrender to the process of knowing what already exists. Let go of all the hooks and Velcro holding us back from expanding. Let go of fear and anger, of knowing and believing. Let go of limits.

As we let go, new areas of growth and opportunity open up. We may want to consolidate our growth and put a special application of will and purpose to use. That special method is the vow.

A vow is another will statement used to help with special areas of growth. When we have a spiritual need that we wish to work with, a vow can provide a path for moving forward. Historically, vows were used by religious orders and other spiritual sects to separate spiritual pursuits from worldly pursuits. You and I will not be using it in that sense.

Bruce Davis, in his wonderful book *Monastery Without Walls*, has an excellent section on vows which I recommend highly. A vow is a special application of the will to help us move into the sacred. It is a will statement used to purify or sanctify a purpose with total commitment. Monks and nuns in the past have taken vows of poverty, charity, chastity, and so on. We take marriage vows. We swear vows of loyalty.

A vow places the will in total surrender to the Higher Self and its purpose for that particular activity. A vow of poverty means surrendering totally to the Higher Self and God for material needs. A vow of charity means surrendering totally to a life of service. When we are ready to make vows, it means we surrender to the nobleness and sacredness in our purpose, or that part of our purpose, and will to make it inviolate.

Poverty

I, Todd Weber, a child of God, vow to empty myself to make each day, each meal, each breath, each possession I enjoy, each person in my life, and each experience I receive fully

*appreciated and not taken for granted. I will
remember that* **everything** *is given as a gift.*

That vow of poverty is an expression of moving into
poverty of the spirit, of accepting each precious moment as
a gift and appreciating it fully. It is not a statement of material
deprivation. I do not need to suffer to grow spiritually;
neither do you. This vow imbues a segment of my purpose
with sacredness. I vow to accept each moment as a gift, a
sacred moment, each and every one.

I use vows for a short period of time to spur my awareness. We can make vows for three months, a year, or a
lifetime. It is a matter of where we want to place special
emphasis on our growth and the nature of its direction.

Chastity

*I, Todd Weber, a child of God, vow to be
connected to the fidelity that joins me to God.
Through the true love of my partner and the
true love of my community, I vow to touch
the purity of God's unconditional love.*

Chastity is not necessarily celibacy. My vow is to be
joined with God through my partner. By remaining in *faith*
and *trust* with my partner, I reaffirm the fidelity of my bond
to God. Celibacy can be a way of avoiding the sexual
expression of spiritual love, and denying the beauty of that
expression. Celibacy can also be used as a spiritual tool,
however, in line with the concept of chastity.

Can you see the difference between a will statement and
a vow? It is a method of placing honor, respect, and
sacredness on ourselves and our purpose. It moves us into
a new dimension of will and purpose. It carries tremendous
force. Do not make a vow lightly. Use the will to move
powerfully into the next level of spiritual development, and
trust in the process to help surrender to its flow.

Charity

*I, Todd Weber, a child of God, vow to live my
life as a gift to be given to all I touch. I*

*surrender to serving a life that moves toward
God and helps in removing the obstacles
from others' paths. I vow to give myself
totally in gratitude and love that reflects my
desire to be an instrument of God's love.*

In placing myself in total surrender to these parts of my purpose, I let go of all hooks and hindrances to my growth. God gathers me up in His arms and cradles me in the sacredness of my vow. We can move and expand without limit by using the will to move into the spiritual dimension.

Not everyone will want to take a vow, even a short-term one. A vow conveys a sense of commitment and reverence that must be taken with the heart. It is so powerful because of the unspoken agreement that the universe and our Higher Self enter to complete the intent. All of nature and the spirit unite in supporting the intent of the vow. It is the highest use of the will.

In surrendering to the intent or purpose of the vow, we allow God to make us bigger. We gain more room for the vastness and glory of the universe to pour into and out of the vessel of our hearts. We become purer and more whole from the experience. We have more to give and share. It is an accelerated expansion into the flow, where it is easiest to surrender to the growth and let the assimilation and integration of the experience catch up later.

Here are a few of the areas where vows might be useful. Vows are taken in context to a relationship—our relationship to the world, to others, to God, to the church, to a spouse. A vow is a commitment to move that relationship into the sacred, toward the holy, into total surrender to the purpose, into total acceptance of the love and grace and gratitude intrinsic in every relationship.

Vows guide the spiritual life of the soul. Each vow opens another area of growth to the unlimited love of God and the bounty of the universe.

Spiritual vows of poverty have guided Christian and Buddhist monks and mystics for centuries. In Hinduism, it is called the path of emptiness. It is a life of detachment, of stewardship. In making a spiritual vow of poverty we are moving through life with the empty hands of the spirit.

A vow of poverty does not mean living without material comforts. It means not being attached, *grasping*, to material possessions or possessions of the heart. Rich or poor, we all have possessions and attachments. A vow of poverty is giving up the attachment to free the spirit.

Chastity is a vow to perfect our love. It does not have to mean celibacy, although that can be a part of it. It is moving into communion with the unconditional love of God through our partner or our community. Chastity is not necessarily a denial of sexuality. Rather, it is an affirmation of the joy and holiness of fidelity and expression of God's love through the body shared with our partner. It is an affirmation of commitment of the spirit which purifies and makes sacred the sexuality and sensuality of our pure love for another.

Chastity reflects receiving and giving love through the shining grace of the unconditional love of God. We can reflect that love in solitude through our love of the spirit, or through a relationship with another. It is a path of strict accountability. A promiscuous and carefree attitude in a relationship is not chaste. Chastity can make every act in a relationship a reverent affirmation of total trust and fidelity, and an expression of God's love through us.

Vows of obedience are not as popular as they once were with the feminist awareness bringing the sexist nature of the vow to light. However, a vow of obedience in a spiritual context can be very helpful. It can be a promise to surrender to the true authority of God and our Higher Self working through us. It can bring us into contact with our true purpose and our surrender to it: obedience to our true calling, gratitude, and talent.

Most of us rebel from commitment. We lack trust. We hedge against fully surrendering. We fear lack of control or ego death. With obedience, we surrender to our inclination to grow and expand spiritually. We find our true home in the universe of unconditional love and grace.

Charity is another traditional vow in religious orders. The vow of charity is a call to service, a surrender to the flow of gifts from God and becoming a conduit to pass those gifts on to others.

Again, Mother Teresa is a great example of a vow of charity in action. Her love and God's love become the perfect gift to uplift and help others. Charity is not how *much* we give, but the *quality* of the love we give and the *gratitude* in being able to give. A vow of charity is a promise to detach ourselves from the results of the giving and become totally involved in the act of giving itself. It is the sacred surrender of the gift of our life to others.

Marriage vows and personal vows are other forms used to remind and commit us to the sacred in our lives. We can design vows for any purpose. They are the ultimate use of the will and are very powerful.

Try writing out some vows for a few areas of your life. Use the vows in this book or others as models for your own. When you are satisfied with your vow, then make a simple ceremony where you commit to it. It can be a short-term or a lifetime commitment. Read your vows every day.

Without living our new purpose and commitment, it is without meaning—and that is The Next Step.

Lifestyle

The great use of life is to spend it for something that will outlast it.
—William James

The Next Step in moving into a larger life is designing a lifestyle that incorporates the magnitude of our purpose, a way of living that balances the emotional, physical, mental, and spiritual aspects into a matrix of growth and sharing.

We will examine each area of lifestyle to explore the potential for designing a way of living that reflects the nobility and dignity of our purpose. We will place it all into the context of relationships, for it is in a relationship that our personal growth and expansion is tested and refined through the day-to-day reality of living with others.

Relationships with a partner or spouse are the most demanding and special gifts we receive. A partner sees us when we don't have our makeup on, and when we are grouchy and irritable. A partner sees us in the process of growth, not just the finished or polished aspects of it. A partner is also on the journey of growth, and has separate issues of resistance that may conflict with ours. Ken Keyes, Jr. speaks very eloquently in his books about the special nature of the growth possible in relationships, and the conflict of unresolved addictions.

Without the resistance of my second wife, I would never have progressed as quickly as I did. The rough mirror of my process that she provided gave me the direction and impetus for growth. A loving partner can do more for providing the material for constructing a masterpiece of a life than any other way I know. That is what we are doing here, designing and constructing a masterpiece, a glorious and full life that reflects the unconditional love and grace of God and the unlimited potential of man.

In a loving relationship with a partner, we can explore all aspects of spiritual communion and intimacy. Through the true love of a partner we experience directly the love of God. We experience the fidelity of love in context with spiritual growth. We test our expansion and purpose through the friction provided by living with someone on a day-to-day basis. We continue to grow through the practice of gratitude and the realization that all experience is a gift. By sharing our gifts, we expand into being capable of receiving more, which allows us to give more, and so on.

A partner can be the most important tool for growth we have. This can also be the hardest area for us to put our growth into practice. Share with your partner the purpose and direction of your growth and help each other to expand and enlarge in order to become capable of more. It is the greatest gift we can give to each other.

Sex in a relationship is another area where fantastic growth can occur. Between loving partners committed to a spiritual path, sex (or making love, which is actually more accurate in this situation) can lead to expansion of the spirit.

In our society, we are so sexually repressed that pornography, sadomasochism, X-rated movies, and so on actually have a market. We are taught as children to deny our sexuality and pretend it doesn't exist. Not until puberty, when the hormones are raging out of control, are we allowed to begin expressing our sexuality, and then we must do it in hiding. It is illicit to show love, affection, and caring outside of a "legitimate" relationship.

If you come from a dysfunctional family, like I did, then the sexual roles and expressions are even more restrictive and distorted. I highly recommend getting counseling and reading in this area if you have anxiety and concern about your sexual identity and role. A spiritual relationship is a safe place to work through these issues and grow into the unlimited children of God we are.

Placing our relationships on spiritual grounds allows us to surrender into the reflection of God's love and its perfect mirror in our bodies. The tantric yoga of sex always confused me until I came to this understanding, that the human body is the perfect instrument of God's love and that the sexual union is the highest use of that body to move into God, through the fidelity and love of a partner. When we release the sexual conditioning of our family history and society and move into a spiritual communion with our partner, it becomes one more path to express our desire to know and melt into God.

A loving partner, in concurrence with our purpose, is the perfect path and teacher to higher spiritual realms. The solitary spiritual seeker is denied the depth and texture of God's love reflected in an intimate relationship and loses some of the advantages of having a loving mirror reflecting the areas of growth. However, a solitary seeker doesn't have to deal with the resistance of a partner, either. There are other advantages to the solitary path, which can lead to accelerated expansion also.

Examine your purpose in light of your relationships and discover the context in which sharing and giving gain extra depth and meaning in intimacy. The nature and form of the relationship can change over the years as both partners grow and expand, but that intimate connection will never break when taken in light of a spiritual path.

A relationship is where we determine the nature of our growth and reflect the commitment to the next step in evolving as a spiritual being. All else that we will discuss in terms of a spiritual lifestyle must be placed in terms of a relationship. Even if you are single, and not involved in an intimate partnership, your relationship with God and the universe is reflected in your lifestyle, and how you relate to all other beings you contact in life.

The Next Step is devising a life that is purposeful. That purpose will be reflected in all areas. In practicing gratitude, and surrendering to the flow, it soon becomes apparent that our connection to the Higher Self is a constant and thrilling experience. In that connection, we discover the symbols and signs of our purpose. Our lives become the expression of those symbols.

By surrendering to our purpose, power is gained to express it. One of the aspects of a meaningful purpose and expressing it is giving or sharing. A spiritual lifestyle always contains sharing. A hallmark of a conscious being is generosity: of finances, time, possessions, appreciation, praise, and credit.

We discussed generosity of finances when we looked at prosperity. The spiritual lifestyle is prosperous. We live in an unlimited universe, where the giving of those things we are allowed to steward expands the area of stewardship. Some say a minimum expression of that is tithing 10% of net income, but it is more than putting a set number or percentage on the amount of money we are willing to share or give away. It is an opening of the spirit that sees the connection between us all and acknowledges that to limit one of us is to limit all of us.

Expressing our generosity through sharing money is a concrete action toward expanding the spirit. It is a way of taking a step on the path. It is both the means and the ends. Money and prosperity are limited yardsticks that we can use to mirror our spiritual growth. How attached are you?

Generosity is grounded in gratitude and love, as is all spiritual expansion. The practice of gratitude places us in the now. In the now, the potential is limitless. It is all there to share. The perspective and detachment of gratitude allows us to see the sharing in context with the flow. The more we share, the more the unlimited nature of the universe is revealed.

Learn to use your Higher Self as a source of help and guidance, especially when faced with issues that are hindering or slowing expansion of the spirit. Gratitude is the fastest way to the Higher Self and that connection with God.

Financial generosity, and the lack of it, is just one indication of any hindrances or hang-ups we may still have in connection with money and prosperity. "Ask and you shall receive. Knock and the door shall be opened." Know that the other side of that is to be asked to give, and to have someone knock is to open to the experience.

In our culture, time is the most treasured commodity. We guard and are jealous of our time. Generosity of time is another indication of sharing the spirit. To whom do you give your time? Where do you "spend" time? As we discussed about prosperity, our time has value in the marketplace, based on the worth we place on it. Our time has value spiritually, also. That value is based on how we use our time in pursuit of our purpose. Is our purpose noble? Does it include sharing with others? Then part of the pursuit of our purpose will include giving time to others.

That does not necessarily mean we spend time directly in service to others. Your purpose may be a solitary means of providing a method that will benefit many others with its application. Only you can be the judge of that. However, generosity of time is more than giving time to our purpose. It means being available to those we love; to ourselves, when quiet thought or contemplation is necessary; and to others when they have need.

Also, generosity of time may mean to tithe time as we do with finances in order to discipline spiritual growth and intent. Give time as a volunteer to your community, church, or organization. Spend time giving to someone else's purpose. Tithe time as a symbol of humility and spiritual opening, and to serve as a gesture of the availability of your spirit. For some, this is the most important and symbolic action to take in opening to the spirit.

Generosity of time is a hallmark of the conscious being. An amazing thing happens when we open to sharing our time. Just as happens with finances, the more time we share, the more time expands and becomes available to us. Energy becomes available that wasn't there before. Sharing time with someone in need is its highest use, and the spirit provides in the sharing.

Become aware of the higher use of your time in pursuit of your purpose and in being available, in love and gratitude, to those who need "your time."

Sharing possessions is another indication of the generosity of the spirit. The old saying, "my house is your house" is more than a statement of welcome. It is an affirmation of the fact of stewardship. God owns it all. We are only managers of it. To grasp and hold possessions in greed and need is to deny the spiritual connection of the material to God, and the unlimited nature of the universe.

A friend and I were out to lunch and she questioned me on the "unlimited" nature of the universe. She said she thought that a lot of our current and future difficulties were based on a planet with limited resources and a people who have not managed those resources wisely. We are beginning to pay the price for that neglect, and will pay more heavily in the future.

I agreed that the planet is in difficulty due to bad stewardship of the resources provided, and that unless major shifts in consciousness happen quickly, the rain forests will be gone and the pollution and waste situation will be overwhelming. Then I asked her a simple question. Given the current trend in stewardship, what is the fastest growing resource available? She answered "waste." I agreed.

There is unlimited opportunity in using, processing, refining, and recycling waste. Our economic base is going to have a major shift in the not too distant future as we move from a natural resource based economy of oil, wood, gas, etc. to an economy based on sunlight, waste resources, and service. It is an unlimited potential. The shift will be painful, but we will have to make it if we are to keep this planet and prosper.

As we discussed in the section on purpose, this planet is in need of people with big ideas, leaders of a higher order than our current crop of politicians. We need leaders who can see the nature of the shifts taking place on the planet and provide the necessary vision to move us into the 21st century. The opportunity is unlimited for those with vision.

Stewardship is a matter of generosity, but not stupidity. We do not open our door to thieves. We keep the wolves from the sheep, but for those in need, we always can make more available. The people of the Navajo Nation have a long tradition of owning no land. It is an example we can all take to heart. The land belongs to God. It all belongs to God and we are the caretakers.

Generosity of spirit is given in appreciation and gratitude for the gifts we receive. A conscious being fully appreciates each day, each experience, and each person for the true miracle of perfection and grace they represent. Living a spiritual lifestyle is an exercise in appreciation and gratitude.

Practicing gratitude daily expands the now into infinity. As Joseph Campbell talked about in his books on mythology, the instant of now is where infinity exists. Gratitude and appreciation keep us in the now. Through an active practice of appreciating each moment, each event, each feeling, we become grounded in the now. The practice of gratitude is also the direct link to our Higher Self, so we become established in the flow of that higher wisdom and vision and make greater use of the now.

A spiritual lifestyle includes sharing praise in accomplishment and effort. We share with and give praise to God and the Higher Self for the help and gifts received, and for all those on the journey.

Seeking recognition and identity through accomplishment and work is just as greedy as hoarding money. The act of grasping and holding praise for results limits the vision of the task. Remember, our control is in our efforts and the results are God's, through the free will of others. Recognition of all effort and contribution is sharing in the bounty of the harvest. Through that sharing the rewards of the spirit are increased. A spiritual lifestyle is open in surrendering to the efforts of all and sharing the recognition and contribution of all. Through generosity of spirit, true freedom is gained.

Being generous is grounded in gratitude and in acknowledging that all we seek in life is already present. Learning to see the good and acknowledging the gifts allows us to open to sharing and giving in abundance. Generosity in all areas of life is acknowledged through expressing the gifts. Notes, cards, flowers, words of praise or comfort, sharing the meaning of value to another are all ways of being generous. It doesn't have to be a material expression. Sharing the spirit is also generous.

A spiritual lifestyle also includes attention to balancing and purifying the body, mind, and spirit. Through our method of living, we can express our purpose and will to expand in the spirit. That method must include balance in all areas of life.

How is a spiritual lifestyle expressed with our bodies? We've already discussed the aspect of sex in a spiritual partnership. Let's examine the total expression of physical being. There are countless books and magazines available on health, diet, and exercise. Our culture is obsessed with beautiful bodies. Youth and thinness are worshipped. We've made dieting a mainstay of our national economy. Salons and plastic surgeons are overbooked.

I am constantly amazed why no one, or very few, asks why dieting is necessary to begin with. What is it that causes overeating and weight problems to begin with? We talked about eating disorders when we discussed anger, and I am sure that is a large part of the problem.

Yet rather than address that problem, it is much easier and more satisfying to go on a diet. Of course, the fact that diets don't work, or very rarely, doesn't seem to make a difference. People don't seem to be able to keep their weight off.

Then there is the other side of the coin—those folks so obsessed with their bodies that they spend all their discretionary time in the gym working on their physique or running, swimming, bicycling, or aerobicizing. Being fit becomes another addiction or obsession; a healthier addiction, perhaps, but out of balance just the same. It makes one wonder exactly what is the perfect balance in maintaining health.

In a spiritual lifestyle, the emphasis is on being a fit temple for God. The body is an overcoat for the soul. "How does my body express my purpose and reflect my commitment to the spirit?" That is a question we all must ponder. It is an individual judgement, but there are a few considerations that we should keep in mind.

First, we must remember that the body, mind, and spirit are all interconnected. Ken Dychtwald, in his book *Bodymind*, discusses his observations of changing the body and seeing the changes in the mind and spirit and vice versa. Dan Millman, in *The Way of the Peaceful Warrior*, gives some beautiful insights to the spirit-body-mind connection through a wonderful metaphorical story. Many of the martial arts are grounded in the discipline of the spirit being the basis for the discipline of the body, and the reverse.

We cannot isolate work on one area of our lives and not have it affect other areas, just as we cannot expect to change ourselves without affecting our relationships in the family system and with others. We are all connected. We are all systems that are interdependent, both internally and externally. We must work in that context, if we are to make lasting changes and growth.

It makes sense to consider the nature of our disciplines. All discipline affects other disciplines. If we are in recovery, it makes sense to look at changing physical patterns in context to the discipline of our program of recovery. If we are not in recovery or in a program, then looking at our current disciplines makes sense. How would changing your body affect the other changes you are making?

If we maintain our program or discipline one day at a time, staying in the now through gratitude, then it seems the best approach to new growth is on the same basis. Do it now, one day at a time. Do the little thing today that moves in the direction you wish to go, and build on it tomorrow. Do it today.

How is a spiritual lifestyle reflected in the body? Some ancient traditions believe that the body must be as pure as possible, without violence associated with the diet. No killing, which means no animal products. No contaminants, which means no smoking, drugs, or alcohol. It is a physical regimen which moves the seeker closer to God.

In this culture, a less rigid approach might prove more helpful: try a diet that reflects health and growth of the spirit as well as the body, perhaps moving lower on the food chain to help in resource management. You might try a reduction in meat and poultry and fish consumption to reflect less violence in the diet, or a diet that allows adjustment for food lovingly prepared by friends and family, even if it doesn't fit our current preferences. It doesn't mean we have to overindulge for the sake of others, but a gentle acceptance of small portions can be a gesture of love.

A spiritual lifestyle is not rigid. Circumstances and the will of others provides many opportunities to reflect unconditional love in the acceptance of changes. When you have control, then stick to your preference for a diet, one day at a time. When you don't have total control, then lovingly accept small portions of food prepared by others. It doesn't have to be a big issue.

There is one exception to this open acceptance. If we are addicted to a food or substance, then to lovingly refuse it is the only course. It can be done in such a way that it does not offend, as can any polite refusal. However, to expect special treatment or individual separate preparations in social situations is not a spiritual approach. Be firm in your discipline, and loving in your acceptance or refusal.

The shape of our bodies is a private decision, but to jeopardize our health through obesity, undereating, bingeing, or purging is not a balanced way of living. It does not reflect a reverence for the body which is the home of God. Whether we decide to become an Adonis or Venus, or we are content to be pleasantly out of shape, is an individual preference. Impairing the health of the temple is not.

There are obviously many other issues besides diet which affect the shape of the body, such as emotions and exercise, but in a spiritual lifestyle the issue of fat or any eating disorder must be addressed.

I have been to many spiritual presentations where the teacher was grossly overweight. I tried valiantly to listen to the message, not the messenger, but it is a truth that the messenger is a validation of the message. If a person is grossly overweight, it will call into question the congruence of every area in that person's life. How can I give total acceptance of the message to someone purporting to be on a spiritual path who cannot gain mastery of this form? It is a matter of living the message—reflecting the inner purpose in outer form.

Our life in every area must reflect our spiritual commitment. If it doesn't, it doesn't mean that we are "bad" or "wrong." It means we need to examine the blocks to our going in that direction and gently move toward the *embodiment* of our purpose and commitment.

With all that is known about how cigarettes and other tobacco products threaten health, not only of the person smoking, but of others in the area, how can a spiritual lifestyle include smoking? It would seem to deny a basic premise of being a loving, giving person. If you still smoke, it is time to give it up. Sure, I know that quitting smoking is harder than kicking heroin, according to the experts. I quit smoking about nine years ago. I did it the same way I quit drinking. I asked for help; I quit one day at a time; and I had a support group of two friends who quit with me.

Smoking, drinking, drugs, eating disorders, obsessive sex, addictive religion, work addiction, exercise addiction, and all other activities or substances used in an obsessive or addictive manner are an indication of a spiritual problem. It may be in terms of family dysfunction, it may be in terms of personality disorder, it may be in terms of misuse of the will. They all become problems of the spirit. With the help of the Higher Self and God, the will can be used in a way to move toward health and spiritual growth. It is a decision and a discipline which needs to be practiced every day, one day at a time.

Which brings us to exercise. Exercise is a discipline, but like all disciplines, there is reward in the doing as well as in the results. Exercise affects more than just the body. Much research documents the beneficial effects of exercise on stress reduction, emotional balancing, and increased self-esteem. The positive effects of exercise, done in balance with the rest of a purposeful life, are great.

There is one more benefit of exercise on the spirit that is not generally acknowledged. Part of the growth in the spirit is that life becomes much more playful. Having a body that can play makes it much easier to express the joy and bliss and lightness of spirit. Exercise is play! It puts us into condition where we can play more fully and completely, as well as being a reflection of the life of the spirit.

Exercise can be a moving meditation. Running provides a delightful opportunity to exercise and meditate at the same time. We are able to **move** with spirit and relax into surrendering to the flow. Some of my best experiences spiritually have been while running and meditating.

Exercise conditions the body, but also liberates the mind and spirit. Increasing the energy available for living and growing is a wonderful pursuit and exercise gives more energy. If you do not have a regular exercise discipline, now is the time to start. The resources for exercising are limitless and easy to find. Get started now.

The body is the temple of the spirit and reflects our condition in much more depth than just physically. Examine your physical reality and decide how closely it matches your purpose. A spiritual lifestyle is a life in the body, interconnected with mind and spirit. The health and condition of one affects the health and condition of all. The Next Step includes a regular, disciplined exercise and nutritional program which reflects the spiritual commitment to growth. (Also see *Lifestyle Changes: 12 Step Recovery Nutrition and Diet Guide*, Glen Abbey Books 1991.)

We tend to live in our heads. We need to reconnect with our bodies. Take yoga classes, movement classes, dancing classes. Integrate the spiritual experience in the body and feel it gain depth. Feel your body respond to the spiritual expansion.

As we grow spiritually, our body moves differently, we hold emotion in the body differently, and our muscles change. We can't change one part of the system without affecting other parts. If you are having difficulty with weight, look at your spiritual program, your emotional program, and your exercise program, as well as your diet, then move toward becoming whole with the spirit.

It is no mistake that the ancient paintings, statutes, and depictions of spiritual beings represented them in perfect human form. Many of the representations show a radiating aura or halo around the figure. The body is the barometer of the spirit and will reflect the realization and attunement with spiritual awareness.

Begin a physical program as a part of your lifestyle, if you don't have one in place. The balancing nature of exercise, good nutrition, and purification of the body is tremendously powerful in helping spiritual pursuits. Take advantage of this miraculous gift of a body and treat it with the sacred trust and responsibility it implies.

The next area to be addressed in a spiritual lifestyle is the mind. Most of this book is about using the mind as an instrument for change. In a spiritual lifestyle there is a regular program of mind development and clean-up. We get ample opportunity to examine our spiritual progress by how we react emotionally in our day-to-day living.

The mind is a marvelous gauge of growth and a tempting maze to explore. We tend to believe our thoughts and feelings are the only reality. We get trapped in that reality and its limited dimensions of our own beliefs, thoughts, experiences, and perceptions. From within that mindset, it is difficult to be aware of blocks to growth and expansion. That is why it is necessary to move to the broader perception of the Higher Self through the use of the will to progress beyond these blocks.

This makes it apparent why a therapist, teacher, friend, or sponsor is necessary when dealing with old tapes and behavior patterns. If you are still hung up on family-of-origin difficulties, please get some help. The energy trapped in those old beliefs and habits of living is great and must be released in order to grow. We are doomed to continue acting out the unresolved issues of family of origin until they are addressed. Usually it will take a trusted therapist or advisor to help us get beyond these issues.

It does not have to be a long-drawn-out, painful process. With the help of the Higher Self and the will, in line with your spiritual progress, you can give a therapist or counselor all that is needed to get immediate help. With the will to release that energy for use in your purpose and spiritual life, the process will accelerate and expand.

Letting go of being right, of opinion, conditions, demands, judgements, criticism, and expectations is a lifetime project. However, with a heartfelt intent to grow past these limitations, progress is immediate and steady. The will is such a marvelous gift. We must explore all the possibilities of using the will. Use it now to help in moving past and through any remaining family-of-origin hooks.

The mind is the instrument of shaping our purpose for expression. Through the use of the will and the Higher Self providing direction, our purpose is defined and explored. It is one of the highest uses for the mind. When we employ our minds in this fashion, all sorts of inspiration and motivation occur that could not be anticipated.

When we let go of judgement, criticism, expectations, and so on, the mind is available as an instrument of discernment and purpose. Rather than labeling experience, belief, and knowledge, the mind sorts and prioritizes based on higher purpose and sharing. Having to name experience as "good" or "bad" or any other label is left behind. The gift or lesson available in each experience, emotion, or bit of knowledge becomes apparent, and the mind is able to discern its current value and store the remainder for future consideration and use.

Higher knowledge is not linear. When we judge experience or perception based on what we know rationally, we miss the potential connections with past or future purpose. In examining the past, how many experiences or awareness seemed to be "tragic" or "sad" or "bad" at the time they occurred, but later, when put into perspective, became very valuable lessons for growth and expansion into your purpose?

A spiritual lifestyle includes examining life for meaning and purpose. The best use of the will is in moving into a noble purpose that expands and enlarges through giving and sharing with others in some form. The mind is a wonderful gift for use in examining meaning, formulating intent and will, expressing purpose, and partaking of all the unlimited opportunities that God and the universe provide.

Part of that lifestyle may be periods of solitude, time spent alone to evaluate, think, and examine purpose and will; time spent in retreat to quiet the everyday needs of the intellect and emotions, and to move the will and mind into alignment with spiritual pursuit.

A spiritual lifestyle requires a spiritual program, a disciplined approach to expanding and becoming, with time spent in solitude for prayer and meditation. Perhaps a religious discipline will be included, or just a simple spiritual practice. To have meaning and impact it must be a discipline, part of the daily routine leading toward the integration of all parts of life as a spiritual expression. Eventually, the spiritual practice transcends separation of the different areas of life and **becomes** life.

Through the practice of gratitude, it is possible to become established in the now. There are many other paths, but the journey is the same, and that journey is just a projection of a place or state of being we already have. Don't be misled by labels or dogma. Use your heart and Higher Self to discern the practice best for you. Surrender to your purpose and the expression of that purpose with God, and let go!

The moment-to-moment flow of life contains the whole of existence. Moving into that realization as an established mode is the fruit of a spiritual lifestyle. Every act becomes a spiritual act. Every moment is a moment of reverence. Every breath becomes a prayer. Every thought becomes an aspiration. Every move becomes a move toward and into God.

To settle for less is to diminish the gifts we've received. To live less fully than the capabilities and talents we've received is to be in defiance of God. To resign from the struggle of becoming because of suffering and pain is to miss the gifts and lessons being offered. Seeing the choice, we must take it! Once we've perceived the potential, anything less is a step into moral bankruptcy.

It is not attainment that is important. *It is effort.* To strive and will with less than full effort means having that small voice in our minds always saying, " I wonder what would have happened if I had given my *all*?" To be able to look at life without regret, but with satisfaction in the effort and intent is the hallmark of a spiritual lifestyle.

Effort is not the key to realization; it is the key to will and purpose. Purpose is an expression of our spiritual intent—picking up the hoe and giving full effort with love. That is where our intent is multiplied with the spiritual resonance to higher meaning.

Could a person looking at your life tell you are following a spiritual path? Does your work reflect a loving and purposeful intent? Do your friends and associates have spiritual interests and expressions active in their lives? Do you have a spiritual teacher or mentor? Does your body mirror a move toward the fitting temple of God it was intended to be? Are your mental and emotional habits reforming into pure, reverent gifts to others that reflect God's unconditional love?

Ask yourself hard questions and examine your life. Decide now to move toward God as a lifestyle, not with just individual activities or acts, but as a way of living. Find a purpose that is big enough to stretch your talents and inclinations and that gives to others. Surrender into that purpose and let the expression of it forge your life. Will to be more, give more, have more, reflect more, and open to the flow of God's love and gifts. The Next Step is yours to take.

The Next Step

Living **beyond** steps, programs, teachings, and dogma is the ultimate step. Learning to express fully the spiritual potential we are born with and sharing it with others becomes a way of living.

The Next Step requires work, will, and purpose. It requires discipline to act today. The Next Step is a surrender to the larger meaning of our lives and moving to expand it to the utmost.

Practicing gratitude to become grounded in the now, forgiving and releasing those hooks and entanglements that inhibit growth, and moving toward unconditional love leads to unlimited expression of our purpose.

Challenge yourself and others to go for it! Choose to be more. Choose to give more. Let go of results and give full effort in the purpose. Choose to be a truly unlimited child of God.

There are still issues and problems in an unlimited life, but there are no filters to experiencing those issues and problems. An unlimited life offers many gifts and lessons. Expanded awareness and experience of the flow give new perception to every emotion, experience, and insight. The process of expansion accelerates and intensifies with each new level of surrender. Use your will to come home to God. Use your purpose to share the homecoming!

The choice is yours.

Recommended Reading

Anonymous — *The 12 Step Prayer Book* (Glen Abbey Books, Inc., 1990). A collection of favorite 12 Step prayers and inspirational readings.

Davis, Bruce, Ph.D. — *Monastery Without Walls* (Celestial Arts, 1990). An exploration into silence and its place in our lives.

Dychtwald, Ken — *Bodymind* (Jeremy P. Tarcher, 1977). A good primer on the wholeness of body, mind, and spirit.

Keyes, Ken Jr. — *The Power of Unconditional Love* (Love Line Books, 1990). Guidelines for improving or changing your meaningful relationships.

Levine, Stephen — *A Gradual Awakening* (Anchor Press/Doubleday, 1979). A wonderful, gentle book that introduces a breathing meditation.

Millman, Dan   *The Way of the Peaceful Warrior* (H.J. Kramer, Inc., 1980). An allegorical story with some very good lessons.

Rama, Swami   *Living with the Himalayan Masters* (Himalayan International Institute of Yoga Science and Philosophy, 1976). A good introduction into Raja Yoga by one of its greatest teachers.

Rollins, Marilyn   *Lifestyle Changes: 12 Step Recovery Nutrition and Diet Guide* (Glen Abbey Books, Inc., 1991). A good basic guide to proper nutrition and the importance of healthy eating and exercise in recovery.

Stauffer, Edith, Ph.D. *Unconditional Love and Forgiveness* (Triangle Publishers, 1987). A wonderful explanation and method for forgiving others and self.

Tulku, Tarthang   *Skillful Means* (Dharma Publishing, 1978). An introduction into Tibetan Buddhism philosophy and the meaning of work.

About the Author

Todd Weber is a Ph.D. candidate in Psychology. He maintains a private counseling practice in the Seattle area, where he also instructs at community colleges, and teaches workshops throughout the Northwest. Todd consults for a number of recovery centers and teaches continuing education for professionals dealing with recovery issues.

For information on workshops, tapes, or seminars:

Todd A. Weber
P.O. Box 3225
Kirkland, WA 98083

Inquiries, orders, and requests for
catalogs and discount schedules
should be addressed to:

Glen Abbey Books, Inc.
P.O. Box 31329
Seattle, Washington 98103

Toll-free 24-hour
Order and Information Line
1-800-782-2239
(All U.S.)